RICHARD FORD AND THE ENDS OF REALISM

The New American Canon

The Iowa Series in Contemporary Literature and Culture

SERIES EDITOR | Samuel Cohen

RICHARD FORD AND THE ENDS OF REALISM

Ian McGuire

*

University of Iowa Press, Iowa City

University of Iowa Press, Iowa City 52242

www.uiowapress.org
Printed in the United States of America
Design by April Leidig

The University of Iowa Press is a member of Green Press Initiative and is committed to preserving natural resources.

Printed on acid-free paper

Library of Congress Cataloging-in-Publication Data
McGuire, Ian.
Richard Ford and the ends of realism / Ian McGuire.
pages cm.—(New American canon)
Includes bibliographical references and index.
ISBN 978-1-60938-343-5 (pbk), ISBN 978-1-60938-344-2 (ebk)
1. Ford, Richard, 1944—Criticism and interpretation. I. Title.
PS3556.O713Z75 2015
813'.54—dc23 2014038708

For Abigail, Grace, and Eve

CONTENTS

ACKNOWLEDGMENTS

Thanks to my colleagues at the University of Manchester's Centre for New Writing for their friendship and intellectual support during the years I have been working on this project, in particular Kaye Mitchell and John McAuliffe, who read and commented on early versions of the manuscript.

Thanks to Richard Ford for his graciousness and generosity in responding to my questions about his work.

Thanks to my editors, Sam Cohen and Elisabeth Chretien, for their consistent support and encouragement during the process of revising and refining the manuscript.

Earlier versions of chapters 2, 3, and 4 appeared in the following journals: chapter 2 in the *Mississippi Quarterly* 65, no. 2 (Spring 2012): 259–80; chapter 3 in the *Journal of the Short Story in English* 60 (Spring 2013): 129–45, copyright 2013 by Presses de l'Université d'Angers, reprinted with permission; chapter 4 in *Textual Practice* 2014, DOI: 10.1080/0950236X.2014.955817.

The Cindy Sherman photographs in chapter 4 are reproduced by courtesy of the artist and Metro Pictures, New York.

INTRODUCTION

"This Balancing of Urgent Forces"

Richard Ford's Pragmatic Realism

This book is, among other things, a defense of contemporary realist writing. I wish to argue that realism remains useful and necessary as a critical category and that contemporary realism, rather than being merely conventional or reactionary, can offer its proponents an aesthetically and philosophically sophisticated way of engaging with and contesting the particularities of contemporary, even postmodern, experience. Before I begin to build those arguments, however, I will first describe and then briefly sketch the history of the arguments I am working *against*, arguments that are still widely accepted, I believe, but whose pedigree and implications are, perhaps, not always fully recognized.

One familiar way of responding to the persistence of literary realism, to the fact that recognizably realist novels continue to be written, published, and read, even though the social conditions and intellectual tendencies that gave rise to realism as a new and distinct literary movement in the nineteenth century have long since receded, is to understand realism as a residual, even a nostalgic, form that harks back to an earlier era in which "reality" was a relatively straightforward thing. Contemporary literary realism, this interpretation suggests, is a vestigial phenomenon, a premodernist hangover, that, while it made perfect sense in the nineteenth and early twentieth centuries, has since then been superseded by more sophisticated modernist and postmodernist techniques that emerge from and are thus far better suited to the newer historical and social conditions. From this perspective, the fact that realism persists even into the twenty-first century functions mainly as a reminder of the unfortunate conservatism and backwardness of much mainstream Anglo-American culture, since to practice realism in the postmodern or even late postmodern age, such arguments go, is by and large a symptom of false consciousness, a sign that the writer, rather than contesting or transgressing ideological orthodoxy, has become entangled in it.[1]

Such antirealist ideas are certainly not new. They have their roots in the founding texts of literary modernism: in the essays of T. S. Eliot and Virginia Woolf and in the promodernist side of the great realism versus modernism debates of the 1930s and 1940s involving Lukács, Bloch, Adorno, Benjamin, and Brecht.[2] Eliot, Woolf, and Adorno, despite their widely differing political viewpoints, all share the belief that a decisive historical break has taken place during the first part of the twentieth century and that realism is no longer adequate to the task of responding to contemporary experience. Woolf's famous assertion that human character changed "on or about December 1910" is offered in "Mr Bennett and Mrs Brown" as part of her larger argument against the inherited tools and conventions of realist writing. "Those tools are not our tools," she goes on, "and that business is not our business. For us those conventions are ruin, those tools are death." Eliot in his 1923 review of *Ulysses* suggests similarly that "the novel is a form which will no longer serve" and that the novel (by which he surely means the realist novel) in fact "ended with Flaubert and James." Adorno argues that, in an era dominated by the culture industry, the role of art is not to represent reality but rather to stand apart and offer an alternative to it. As he explains in *Aesthetic Theory*, "By being different from the ungodly reality, art negatively embodies an order of things in which empirical being would have its rightful place."[3] Seen from this Frankfurt school perspective, realism's mimetic pretensions appear either spurious (the "boy meets tractor" novels of Soviet era orthodoxy) or banally conformist (Hollywood movies and airport fiction).

In the United States in the postwar period, the conservative, Eliotic strain of antirealism finds its most important expression in the work of the New Critics, with their emphasis on aesthetic autonomy and their attachment to lyric poetry, while the more progressive or Romantic versions are articulated through the Marcusean New Left of Ihab Hassan, Leslie Fiedler, Norman O. Brown, and others, with its countervailing emphases on literary experimentation, popular culture, and the liberating power of the irrational. Standing somewhere to the side of these two tendencies, fully agreeing with neither and representing, in consequence, a kind of prorealist *arrière garde*, are the New York Intellectuals (Trilling, Kazin, Howe, etc.), sympathetic to literary modernism, well aware of the Freudian unconscious, yet nonetheless retaining their Old Left beliefs in the novel as a form of social commentary.

The rise of postmodernism and poststructuralism in the late seventies and eighties added powerful new philosophical and sociohistorical elements to the antirealist argument. The post-Saussurean linguistic turn extended and refined an already existing modernist critique of representation and language, and critics like J. Hillis Miller lost no time in showing that even the great nineteenth-century works of realism were in some sense themselves antirealist.[4] It fell to Gerald Graff in *Literature against Itself*, his bracing defense of realism published in 1979, to present the opposing view. Graff, following, broadly speaking, the Left/liberal line of Howe and Trilling, sees New Criticism, literary poststructuralism, and sixties cultural radicalism as all being part of "the general revolt against empiricism which characterizes modern intellectual history." In their anxiety to escape from the instrumentalism and reification of contemporary society, such critics go too far, he argues, and identify reason itself, rather than the particular uses to which reason has been put, as the problem. For New Critics, cultural radicals, and deconstructionists alike, according to Graff, "taking account of objective reality is identified with passive adjustment to the status quo, with the mass man's drugged acceptance of his status as a manipulable object."[5]

In the U.S. academy of the early 1980s, Graff's uncompromisingly prorealist intervention sparked a series of fierce debates over the politics of literary representation that rehearsed in intriguing, if largely unconscious, ways the realism versus modernism battles played out by Lukács, Adorno, and others forty or fifty years earlier (with Graff taking on the role of Lukács). *Literature against Itself* drew vigorous and outraged rebuttals from Jane Tompkins, Alan Wilde, Michael Sprinker, Rodolphe Gasché, W. J. T. Mitchell, and Paul Bové, who denounced its arguments as arrogant, meretricious, dangerous, and parasitic, while Graff, in turn identifying himself with an authentic Leftism, accused his many detractors of practicing an irrational and potentially fascistic pseudopolitics.[6]

Thirty years on, in our current post-postmodern environment and with the passing of the era of high theory, much of the heat has gone out of these arguments.[7] But if antirealism has lost a good deal of its previous vigor, this does not indicate that it has disappeared as a tendency. Rather, I would argue, it has become in modified and muted form incorporated as an element of the critical mainstream. The kinds of frontal assaults on the "referential illusion" undertaken by Roland Barthes or Hayden White may be in the past, in other words, but a certain suspicion of realism as a mode associated with epistemological closure remains.[8] Joe Cleary has recently noted this lingering tendency (and its sometimes detrimental effects) in regard to postcolonial studies, and it is possible to sense a similar antimimetic bias in recent developments in affect theory that associate the real primarily with what is nonobjective and unrepresentable.[9] Even within contemporary trauma theory, which appears to insist, in the face of postmodern skepticism, on the reality of history and of the body, there is a tendency, as exemplified by the de Manian theories of Cathy Caruth, to assume that such realities are literally and metaphorically unspeakable and can only be adequately rendered, therefore, via the kind of literature that foregrounds its own partiality and incompleteness.[10]

It is not my intention in this book to argue that contemporary critics can or should proceed as if modernism never happened or as if the theoretical work of the last forty years has been entirely without value or influence. It would be naive, if not absurd, in our post-Kantian, post-Wittgensteinian context to imagine that our knowledge of the world is ever unmediated or unproblematic. I do, however, want to argue that it is better to understand contemporary realism as a useful way of responding to such problems than as an attempt to evade them. The current persistence of low-level antirealist assumptions, when combined with a dominant model of literacy periodization that sees realism as primarily a late nineteenth-century phenomenon, has created a situation in which the important work of contemporary realist writers is too often ignored or misrecognized by literary critics.

These are broad claims to be sure, and the field of contemporary literary studies is too wide and varied for there not to be some exceptions to them. Realism, as I have already suggested, has always had its champions, but, over the last thirty years, in the academy at least, such critics have been in a minority. Recent defenders of realism such as Robert Rebein and Joseph Dewey have had a relatively small impact on discussions of contemporary literature, whereas the most important and influential critics have tended to follow an antirealist line.[11] For further evidence of this, we may look briefly at the recent work of Fredric Jameson and Mark McGurl, two significant and highly visible critics, one now in the latter stages of what has been a celebrated career, the other the author of what is, by some distance, the most strikingly original recent account of contemporary American fiction.

Jameson did not (of course) invent or discover the narrative of literary and cultural history that sees realism being replaced by modernism, and modernism in turn being replaced by postmodernism (shifts associated in Jameson's Marxist paradigm with the developmental stages of capitalism), but his book *Postmodernism, or the Cultural Logic of Late Capitalism* surely did more than any other recent work to broadcast and solidify that narrative and to attach it clearly and convincingly to a parallel narrative of socioeconomic change. Although Jameson is very much alive to the perils of periodization and does not suggest in *Postmodernism* or elsewhere that realism simply stops after the development of modernism, he makes it plain that by the early decades of the twentieth century realism's most important and defining work is done. He notes, for example, in *The Political Unconscious* (1981) that the realist novel is part of a "bourgeois cultural revolution . . . whereby populations . . . are effectively reprogrammed for life and work in the new world of market capitalism."[12] He continued in the same vein thirty years later in *The Antinomies of Realism* (2013), in which he suggests that "in a stylistic and ideological sense, the consumerism of late capitalism is no longer a bourgeois society . . . and no longer knows the forms of daily life that emerged in the eighteenth and nineteenth centuries: so that realism inevitably gives way to modernism insofar as its privileged content has become extinct."[13]

In this context, the realist fiction that continues to be written after the advent of modernism (what Jameson calls "realism after realism" or "the existential novel") becomes, perhaps not surprisingly, the object of his scorn. He notes at one point in *The Antinomies of Realism* that after the late work of Henry James a "parting of the ways" occurred, with the "serious" writer turning to modernism, while realism rapidly devolved into a form of "easy reading" characterized by "facile free association" and "self-indulgent streams of consciousness."[14] Jameson's attacks on contemporary realism are notable both for their vigor and for their complete lack of specificity: he offers no textual examples and names no names. Whereas his readings of nineteenth-century realist writers (Balzac, Zola, Tolstoy, Eliot) are detailed and respectful, he feels free, by implication at least, to characterize realism's twentieth-century proponents en masse as examples of realism's "shrivelled posterity."[15]

The recent work of Mark McGurl, while quite different from Jameson's in tone and overall method, suggests, if anything, an even more striking lack of interest in or awareness of contemporary realism. While Jameson (even though he dislikes the consequences) accepts that a recognizable form of realism continues on after modernism, McGurl in *The Program Era* proceeds in large part as though realist writing no longer exists. The story of *The Program Era*, and therefore by implication the story of postwar American literature according to McGurl, is the story of the transformations undergone by literary modernism when it engaged with the university via the development of creative writing programs (what McGurl calls "The Fall into Institutionality"). McGurl accepts entirely, it seems, the standard argument that modernism wiped out realism, and he makes his claim for originality on the basis of his description of what happened next. Surveying the field of postwar American writing, he replaces the catch-all term "postmodernism" with a new tripartite taxonomy consisting of high-cultural pluralism, technomodernism, and lower-middle-class modernism. What is most striking about this work, from my perspective anyway, is that realism has no part to play in this story: realism as a term does not appear in the book's index, and even when McGurl engages with specifically realist work (in his excellent discussions of Raymond Carver) he redefines it as a form of modernism. It is perhaps testament to McGurl's considerable skill and verve as a critic that the peculiarity of this procedure—whereby realism, a form of writing that is actually central to most creative writing pedagogy, is entirely ignored in a book dedicated to examining the influence of creative writing programs on American fiction—is only very occasionally apparent. When, in a footnote to one of his many explanatory diagrams, McGurl notes that his binary opposition minimalism versus maximalism implies a third term and then invents, almost in passing, the category of "fine writing" to describe this "neo-classical position" ("one thinks here," he writes, "of the line leading from Fitzgerald through Stegner to John Updike—fine writers all, neither self-effacing nor overbearing"), the reader briefly glimpses another rather different way of describing the landscape of postwar American fiction, but it is a glimpse only, and the category of "fine writing" is never mentioned again.[16]

As I have already indicated, it is my intention in this book to push against the antirealist implications of much contemporary criticism. My purpose in doing this is not to reignite the old realism versus modernism versus postmodernism debates. I am less interested in arguing that realism is *better* than other kinds of writing than I am in pointing out that important realist work continues to be written but that we seem currently to lack the critical tools or the critical inclination to properly engage with it. Exactly *why* realist works continue to be written is of course an interesting and important question also, and, although it is not one I can answer completely here, since to do so would require a much larger and more historically and theoretically oriented book, it is worth noting briefly at the outset, even at the risk of seeming to beg a number of other questions, that my arguments imply that the work the realist novel was contrived to do ("the investigation of reality and illusion" in Lionel Trilling's very simple, but still suggestive, formulation) is, contra Jameson and others, not completed yet.[17]

In the chapters that follow, my larger arguments about realism's continuing importance will be pursued, directly and indirectly, via a series of detailed readings of the works and career of one exemplary and, I would argue, highly significant and previously undervalued postwar American realist: Richard Ford.[18] In my account, the originality and interest of Ford's realism derive not from its well-known but finally unhelpful association with the minimalist or "dirty realist" school of Carver, Tobias Wolff, Anne Beattie, and others but rather from its previously unexplored associations with another but very different intellectual trend of the American 1980s: the revival of American pragmatist thinking as evidenced in the work of Richard Rorty, Hilary Putnam, and their students and followers working in philosophy and other contiguous disciplines. Ford practices, I want to argue, in his novels and short stories a form of *pragmatic realism* in which the traditional realist claims to represent or grasp reality are maintained and indeed developed but are also carefully tempered by a pragmatic, antifoundationalist awareness that any reality that the realist grasps is only ever temporary and that any act of grasping is only ever partial. Ford's realism is in this sense inherently modest in its claims, but it is also inveterately hopeful—there *is* a truth, it suggests, a truth that exists and can be usefully distinguished from error, even if that truth does not have timeless metaphysical foundations.

Ford's pragmatism, which echoes (but does not completely coincide with) that of Rorty and Putnam, is rooted most significantly in his long-standing enthusiasm for Emerson, whom he has described in interview as "the patron saint of novelists" and whose ideas are referred to directly and frequently throughout Ford's Bascombe trilogy.[19] That Emerson is a protopragmatist, possibly even the father of American pragmatism, is a very well known, if still occasionally controversial, claim and one that I will therefore not spend any time justifying here.[20] On the other hand, the claim that a pragmatist philosophy derived from Emerson, William James, and John Dewey can be associated with realism in such a way that "pragmatic realism" can become a useful and meaningful term is much less obvious and requires, as a result, a little more explanatory work. While the antirealist assumptions I have described encourage the belief that literary realism as a mode is naively representationalist, the pragmatist revival of the 1980s and 1990s inspired by the work of Richard Rorty and then developed in slightly different form in the work of literary critics such as Richard Poirier, Jonathan Levin, and Ross Posnock has led to pragmatism being understood primarily as a form of linguistic skepticism and therefore associated with modernism or postmodernism rather than with realism.[21] In order for "pragmatic realism" to function effectively as a category, therefore, it is necessary to show, first, that realism is, or can be, more pragmatic than has often been thought the case and, second, that pragmatism, in turn, is, or can be, more realistic.

To begin with realism: literary realism can be considered potentially pragmatic to the extent that it questions or doubts the metaphysical basis of the realities that it uncovers—to the extent that it recognizes in William James's words that truth is made and not found.[22] The antirealist critique argues that realism is never able or willing to do this, that it always assumes that reality exists independently, "out there," and that language can satisfactorily, unproblematically, reflect it. There are two main ways of defending realism from such a critique. One is to suggest that realism has *always* been more philosophically sophisticated than its recent critics give it credit for, and the other is to suggest that it has, in the postwar period, *become* more sophisticated. These two arguments are certainly not incompatible. As the recent work of Matthew Beaumont and others has clearly shown, it is a mistake to believe that realism, even in its classic nineteenth-century forms, *ever* assumed a simple or uncomplicated relationship between representation and reality, yet at the same time it is not unreasonable to suggest that recent realist writers may be much more aware of the complications of representation than their nineteenth-century predecessors were, that they have in that sense learned from modernism without becoming fully modernist.[23] In the case of Richard Ford, for example, we can point to the important influences of Faulkner and Hemingway, from both of whom Ford learned important lessons about the powers and limits of language without ever feeling the need to follow either of them down the road of more formal, modernist experimentation. What Ford takes from his more modernist predecessors is, in particular, a sense of the importance of *mystery*, a sense that writing, even realist writing, can never tell the whole or final truth. This extremely suggestive term first makes an appearance in Ford's writing in an important 1983 essay on literary influence where he associates mystery particularly with his early reading of Hemingway: "I also learned that for anyone, at any time, some things that matter can't be told, either because they're too important or too hard to bring to words, and these things can be the subject of stories. I think I learned that first and best reading Hemingway, learned the manners and codes and protocols a story observes when it comes round something it thinks is a consequential mystery."[24]

This idea of mystery, as I will discuss at more length in chapter 1, also plays a crucial role in Ford's first major novel, *The Sportswriter*, where it allows him, through various direct and indirect maneuverings, to begin to define the kind of writing he was then (in the mid-1980s) beginning to attempt and to place that new kind of writing in implicit contrast to both his own earlier work and the work of other writers around him at the time. "For me," Frank Bascombe significantly notes in that novel, "mystery is the crucial part, and in fact the *only* thing I find to have value at this stage in my life."[25] Ford's understanding and valuation of mystery in *The Sportswriter* and elsewhere emerge from and are most likely influenced by a variety of factors, including modernism (Faulkner and Hemingway), Romanticism (Emerson), Catholicism (Flannery O'Connor), and, more broadly, the high-cultural liberalism of Trilling, Saul Bellow, and the other postwar American intellectuals for whom art's moral authority was synonymous with its principled refusal to ever simplify or conclude.[26] While the precise relationship between these various influences certainly remains open to debate, it is clear enough, I think, that they all play some part and that their combined influence helps move Ford toward a form of realism that is a great deal more open-ended and philosophically nimble (less metaphysical and more pragmatic, in other words) than antirealists have tended to believe is likely or possible.

Although this monograph will focus primarily on Richard Ford, it is important to recognize that Ford is not the only contemporary American realist to demonstrate pragmatic tendencies in his work or, indeed, to place the idea of mystery at the heart of his literary practice. In his well-known and much criticized 1996 *Harper's* essay (originally called "Perchance to Dream" and later retitled "Why Bother?"), Jonathan Franzen describes a shift in his own thinking and writing from what he calls "depressive realism" to what he calls "tragic realism." To dig beneath these neologisms (and beneath the sometimes frantic surface contradictions of the essay) is to see Franzen first despairing of and then (with a good deal of relief) turning his back on a kind of writing that seeks to adequately represent and thus, via the accuracy and originality of that representation, *change* society. The first half of Franzen's essay is devoted to a pained and occasionally painful lament for the state of contemporary American culture and, in particular, the way that it has marginalized the serious novelist and made the novelist's traditional task of "social instruction" impossible or irrelevant: "Just as the camera drove a stake through the heart of serious portraiture, television has killed the novel of social reportage. Truly committed social novelists may still find cracks in the monolith to sink their pitons into. But they do so with the understanding that they can no longer depend on their material, as Howells and Sinclair and Stowe did, but only on their own sensibilities, and with the expectation that no one will be reading them for news."[27]

Franzen's examples in this passage (William Dean Howells, Upton Sinclair, Harriet Beecher Stowe) suggest that what he calls the novel of "social reportage" is at heart a version of orthodox realism. Franzen, like the antirealists, recognizes that such a novel is no longer viable, but, unlike the antirealists, he suggests that the answer to this problem is not to abandon realism in favor of postmodernism but rather to intelligently redefine it. As *The Corrections*,

Franzen's 2001 novel, whose difficult beginnings the *Harper's* essay in part serves to explain and illustrate, clearly demonstrates, in the mid-1990s Franzen was banging the drum not for experimentalism or technical innovation but rather for a renewed and, crucially, more modest kind of realism.[28] At the very heart of this newer realism is, as with Richard Ford, the idea of "mystery," a term borrowed in Franzen's case much more explicitly from Flannery O'Connor. What defines tragic realism for Franzen and what makes it important and (albeit in a limited sort of way) effective is above all that it embraces *uncertainty*: "I hope it's clear that by 'tragic' I mean just about any fiction that raises more questions than it answers: anything in which conflict doesn't resolve into cant. . . . Tragic realism preserves the recognition that improvement always comes at a cost; that nothing lasts forever; that if the good in the world outweighs the bad it is by the slimmest of margins."[29]

Franzen's ideas of uncertainty and mystery are not rooted as clearly as Ford's are in an explicitly pragmatic or Emersonian tradition (Franzen indeed confesses at one point to the weaknesses of his own historical understanding, and the essay demonstrates a very limited knowledge of American literature and culture before about 1970), yet despite these differences the two arguments certainly point in a similar direction: toward the viability, or necessity, of responding to postmodern conditions by producing a more limited and more pragmatic form of realism. (*The Corrections* goes on to make this same point dramatically via the humiliations it visits on Chip Lambert, a literary theorist whose Foucauldian take on the world the novel relentlessly mocks.)

If literary realism in the cases of Ford and Franzen, then, has the potential to be more pragmatic than has been previously recognized, does pragmatism as a philosophy have a similar potential to be more realistic? Recent neopragmatist accounts of Emerson, James, and Dewey might suggest not. Such accounts have emphasized pragmatism's antirealist tendencies and downplayed or ignored the elements of their work that suggest that the existence of a concept-independent reality might have any role or impact on the process of pragmatic truth making. Under the direct and indirect influence of French poststructuralism, Richard Rorty and Richard Poirier offer the American pragmatist tradition as an earlier, native form of deconstruction. Emerson, James, and Dewey become, in this reading, poststructuralists *avant la lettre*, dedicated to the elimination of all forms of restriction and limitation, dedicated even, Poirier at one point suggests, to the elimination of the self to the extent that it suggests a kind of limit to the exercise of writerly power.[30]

While such revisionist accounts have been influential and are not without evidential support, they are, at the same time, clearly based on quite selective readings of the original texts. Such partiality is acknowledged and justified by Ross Posnock as being in the spirit of Emersonian appropriation. He notes in *Philip Roth's Rude Truth*: "While the Emerson to be found here is a prophet of possibility, this is admittedly not the whole of Emerson—missing, for instance, are the metaphysician and the transcendentalist. But I conduct my appropriation in an Emersonian spirit."[31] Whether or not one accepts the legitimacy of such critical maneuvers, they suggest at the very least the possibility of positing another equally justified and rather different version of the Emersonian/pragmatist tradition—a version that, while retaining the neopragmatist understanding of the importance of what Emerson calls "power," also gives weight to the balancing or opposing principle, which he calls "form." As he writes in "Experience," "Under the oldest mouldiest conventions, a man of native force prospers just as well as in the newest world, and that by skill of handling and treatment. He can take hold anywhere. Life itself is a mixture of power and form, and will not bear the least excess of either."[32] "Form," like "power," has no very strict definition in Emerson's essays, but the term suggests a general recognition of the circumstantial forces that place limits on individual desire or ambition. Such forces are various—they range from the particular nature of the society we live in, the character of our friends and neighbors, and the demands of work and family to larger historical, biological, and genetic factors. To accept the reality of such limits means, in its most benign form, to accept ourselves as we are and to value or believe in the reality of the people, objects, and ideas that are around us, however limiting, mundane, or trivial they may appear. Form, understood in this sense, opposes both cynicism and fantasy in the name of a realist engagement with what already exists.

Emerson's awareness of limitation, of the fact that in an important sense the world cannot be changed by acts of writerly will, however original or accomplished those acts of will might be, is clearly repeated and reemphasized in the work of his pragmatist successors James and Dewey. In both James and Dewey, an emphasis on truth making as a creative human activity that relies in part on individual acts of intuition or genius is balanced by an equally strong awareness of the external circumstances that affect and hem in any such creative activity. Acts of subjective will or power can only become true if they match what already exists both in the sense of what is objectively in the world and in the sense of the previous truths that human beings have made. William James notes in *Pragmatism*, in answer to accusations that pragmatism means believing whatever is most pleasant or convenient, that, "pent in as the pragmatist more than anyone else sees himself to be, between a whole body of funded truths squeezed from the past and the coercions of the world of sense about him, who so well as he feels the immense pressure of objective control under which our minds perform their operations?"[33]

Dewey makes essentially the same point toward the end of *Experience and Nature* in a passage that offers, in slightly more moderate terms than the original, a recapitulation of Emerson's argument in "Fate": "It is precisely the peculiar intermixture of support and frustration of man by nature which constitutes experience. The standing antitheses of philosophic thought, purpose and mechanism, subject and object, necessity and freedom, mind and body, individual and general, are all of them attempts to formulate the fact that nature induces and partially sustains meanings and goods, and at critical junctures withdraws assistance and flouts its own creatures."[34]

Pragmatic truth making occurs, then, philosophically speaking, always in the context of this awkward give and take, not just between new metaphors and old metaphors, as the neopragmatists recognize, but between expressions of individual desire or will and all the other elements of our experience—other objects, other people, other ideas and possibilities and facts—that may encourage or oppose that desire. It is curious, as historian James Kloppenberg has noted in "Pragmatism: An Old Name for Some New Ways of Thinking?," that this aspect of pragmatic thought has been downplayed both by pragmatism's early detractors *and* by its more recent neopragmatist champions. Defending himself against those early detractors in *The Meaning of Truth*, James vigorously insists that pragmatism is realist, not subjectivist, and that it always assumes the existence and the importance of an external reality with which pragmatic truths must concur. "This is why as a pragmatist," he asserts, "I have so carefully posited 'reality' *ab initio*, and why, throughout my whole discussion I remain an epistemological realist."[35]

The possibility of a pragmatic realism emerges, then, from the intersection of a literary realism that is looser and self-consciously less conclusive than the standard version and a form of pragmatism that is rather more aware of limitation and the factors that *restrict* truth making than the more celebratory recent accounts would have us believe. This, I want to argue, is the philosophical and literary middle ground in which Richard Ford's fiction moves—it is a place of restrictions certainly, but also of possibilities.[36] The name he generally gives to this uncertain but vital territory is *normality*, and normality indeed becomes a key term, perhaps *the* key term, in Ford's work from *The Sportswriter* onward. In literary studies, since Foucault at least, normality and normative thinking have tended to be associated with coercion—what is normal is what is conventional (the Foucauldian logic goes), and what is conventional is always an effect of power. Ford's use of the term, however, is quite different from this. For Ford, the normal is not a dull or default condition shared by most of the population but rather a difficult and precarious emotional balancing act by which both form and power (in their Emersonian senses) can be given their due without either being unduly privileged. Normality, in that sense, is a state of mind that may seem unremarkable but is actually hard to achieve and even harder to maintain. In *Independence Day*, which I take to be Ford's most successful and thus most characteristic work, Frank Bascombe associates "the high-wire act of normalcy" directly with an effort to balance "urgent" but contradictory forces. Returning to Haddam, New Jersey, after some time in Europe, Frank feels both limited and limitless. On the one hand, he experiences a sense of "bright synchronicity" and feels that he is "in a charmed state in which nothing was alien and nothing could resist me if I turned my mind to it," but on the other he recognizes that "everything I then contemplated was limited or at least underwritten by the 'plain fact of my existence': that I was after all only a human being, as untranscendent as a tree trunk, and that everything I might do had to be calculated against the weight of the practical and according to the standard considerations of: Would it work? and, What good would it do for me or anybody?"[37] Becoming normal, Frank explains, means recognizing and somehow bringing into balance both these sets of feelings and ideas, the first of which connects to Emerson's idea of power and the second of which connects to his idea of form. This is Ford's pragmatic realism rendered neatly in microcosm—a sense of possibility combined with and balanced by a necessary sense of restraint, and with that sense of restraint itself being rooted in the deeply pragmatic awareness that what matters most is what works in the world, what William James famously calls the "cash value" of an idea.[38]

The drama of the three Bascombe novels, which I will discuss in chapters 1, 2, and 5, emerges primarily from Frank's efforts to recapture, hold on to, or promulgate these values of normality in circumstances that make that balancing act, which is never easy, especially hard to pull off. It is an awareness of death in particular, as a version of fate, form, or limit, by which Frank is continually beset and unbalanced. In the face of such mortal threats and fears (which take many forms), Frank struggles on occasion to maintain an awareness of human possibility and power. At crucial moments in all three novels Frank slips into a state of despair or near despair, but then, usually with the help of other people, he succeeds in righting himself again. As I will discuss in much more detail in chapter 1, the novels attempt, in this sense, a version of the work of mourning in which loss and death must be dealt with by being placed into a correct relation with the rest of life.

That this is essentially a matter of positioning or composition, of finding the correct relationship between life and death (or meaning and meaninglessness) rather than imagining one as superior or prior to the other, is suggested by Ford's persistent interest in graves and burial as a means by which death can be both remembered and forgotten. *Independence Day*, *The Lay of the Land*, and *Canada* all include as part of their conclusions thoughts of burial and visits, or failed visits, to burial places. In all three cases, the point is to be reminded of death but not to hold it too close. In *The Lay of the Land*, for example, Frank, having failed to find his mother's last house, decides not to try looking for her grave. "'It's enough that I tried to find it,' he suggests. 'She'd think that was good. It's one of the ways life's like horseshoes.'"[39] Similarly, when in *Canada* the protagonist, Dell Parsons, visits the place where as a youth he helped bury two murdered men, the conclusion he draws is that death, if correctly understood (i.e., if not given too much weight or importance), can be absorbed into a larger understanding of life: "I drove us—to the extent memory could lead me—near to the place where we buried the Americans. It's odd how a piece of earth can hold so little of its meaning; though that's lucky, since for it to do so would make places sacred but impenetrable, whereas they're otherwise neither.

Instead it all becomes part of our complex mind to which (if we're lucky) we can finally assent."[40] To imagine death or the place of burial as sacred, this passage suggests, would be to make it immune (impenetrable) to the exercise of Emersonian power; it would be to turn it, in other words, into an absolute. But to hold it more lightly, as Dell suggests is possible (and possibly natural), is to make it available as part of a larger picture in which form and power coexist and interpenetrate. This is Ford's pragmatic version of the end of mourning —not the elimination of loss, nor its transformation into a principle or law, but rather its inclusion (if we are lucky) as one distinct element in the broader field of experience.

In the two short story collections that form the basis of my other two chapters, *Women with Men* and *A Multitude of Sins*, the threats to normality come from a distinctly different direction. The tentative balance between power and form, which Ford defines as normality, is threatened in these collections not by the incursions of form or fate (in the shape of death or accident) but rather by an overemphasis on the opposing quality—individual power. We could say, recalling my description of Ford's work as a form of pragmatic realism, that while the danger in the Bascombe novels is of an excess of realism, the danger in *Women with Men* and *A Multitude of Sins* is of an excess of pragmatism. What I mean by this is that the protagonists of these stories have in following their own (usually sexual) desires lost a sense of the nonsubjective, restricting factors that for James and Dewey hem in any act of individual truth making. Emerson notes in "Experience" that "the wise through excess of wisdom is made a fool," and these characters have in some sense gone too far down the antifoundationalist road; their rejection of restrictive orthodoxies has led them to doubt or downplay the reality of a nonsubjective world containing other people and other objects.[41] The result, psychologically speaking, is narcissism and, philosophically speaking, a form of relativism strongly associated with postmodernity. In opposition to these solipsistic tendencies, the stories frequently feature episodes of violence or death—crude incursions of form into the protagonists' postmodern fantasies of power. The result, however, is not the "balancing of urgent forces" (*ID*, 94) that Ford defines as normality but rather a painful lurching from one extreme to another. The best answer to the excesses of postmodern solipsism and self-regard is not, these stories finally imply, to reassert the priority of a nonlinguistic reality but rather to suggest that, whether or not the solipsists like it or recognize it, they are elements of a larger social whole. One of the important limitations under which we operate, one of the factors that restricts our exercise of individual "power," is the fact that the language we speak, even when we try to be most original or individual, is not of our own devising. It is a social and communal construct. This fact, explored most brilliantly by Ford via the meeting between Matthews and his translator, Madame de Grenelle, in the story "Occidentals" may constitute a blow to our pride, but it also offers us, Ford suggests, another way to be normal. The return to the group or community, like the visit to the burial place, is a consistent feature of Ford's novelistic conclusions. In these short stories, such returns occur very rarely and usually too late; nevertheless, when they do occur they indicate if not the imminent arrival of hope, then at least the direction from which hope might eventually come.

So far I have been suggesting that Ford's pragmatic realism follows the line of Emerson and his pragmatist successors in seeking, in the name of normality, to strike and maintain an effective, if never entirely stable, balance between the opposing claims of power and form. It is necessary to recognize, however, that Emerson (who is, of course, a famously and unashamedly contradictory writer) does not himself always strike such a balance and that Ford's adherence to Emerson is consequently not always entirely or purely (if such an adjective can make sense) pragmatic. At the end of "Fate," for example, Emerson appears to reject the idea of balancing the opposing forces of power and form and suggests instead a variety of other, more traditionally metaphysical ways in which the relationship between these two tendencies might be profitably thought through. What we see in such passages is the persistence of an idealist, transcendentalist Emerson who, as an alternative to the complex and confusing work of dialectics, is ready to fall back on a mystical idea of Oneness in which, if the perspective is broad enough, contraries disappear: "Let us build altars to the Beautiful Necessity which secures that all is made of one piece; that plaintiff and defendant, friend and enemy, animal and plant, food and eater are of one kind. In astronomy is vast space but no foreign system; in geology vast time but the same laws as today."[42]

This idealistic, quasi-religious dimension of Emerson's thinking is largely out of step with the irony and secularism of much or most contemporary thought and writing and tends, even in the work of Emerson's recent admirers, to be downplayed or ignored. Ford, in general, displays little or no interest in monistic, religious answers to the Emersonian dilemmas with which his work engages. However, in *The Lay of the Land*, the final volume of the Bascombe trilogy, published after *Women with Men* and *A Multitude of Sins* and, perhaps more importantly, published and written in the immediate wake of 9/11, he does come close to repeating this transcendentalist gesture, albeit in a significantly muted and modified form. What we see in *The Lay of the Land* is Frank attempting to defend himself against the assaults of fate by, in effect, embracing fate itself as a kind of principle. Although the details and the tone of Frank's embrace are different from Emerson's hymning of "beautiful necessity," the two gestures still have a good deal in common. Both see the discovery of underlying permanence, whether the permanence of eternal law or the permanence of character, as a refuge from the apparent unpredictability of life. Frank's decision to enter what he calls the "Permanent Period," which means deciding on and then accepting who and what he *actually* is, seems to offer itself psychologically as a way of lessening the fear of death, of being ready for it when it arrives, but such reassurance is won only at a cost. At certain points in the novel it becomes clear that embracing fate is quite close to embracing death, which is, in turn, quite close to actually *being* dead. What seems like a protective or defensive gesture may actually be a kind of capitulation. The implications of this are never fully worked out in *The Lay of the Land*, which, although the most intellectually energetic of Ford's novels, is also probably the most intellectually imprecise. The novel flirts persistently with religious, "spiritual," or transcendentalist ideas yet can never bring itself to fully embrace them. Indeed, as I will argue more fully in chapter 5, it includes within itself a persistent undercurrent of pragmatic skepticism that works on a formal and unspoken level to undermine or complicate such ideas. In the end, *The Lay of the Land* ends up not so much arguing for or defending the balancing act of normality as much as enacting such an effort via its own internal uncertainties and shifts of emphasis.

What this enactment points toward (and this is made clearer and more explicit in Ford's most recent novel, *Canada*) is the extent to which the balance of normality is or can be expressed via the compositional balance of a successful work of art or fiction. The artist, Ford tells us in *Canada*, is the person most adept at holding in his or her mind two contradictory but equal truths, but this is certainly not an effort that is unique or particular to the creation of art. Here, perhaps, is one final insight into Ford's realist practice—the notion that the work of fiction may be effectively a model for the kind of complex psychological balancings that are required of all of us all the time.[43] Ford's novels and stories become, if understood in this sense, very much like Emerson's essays: they are not only representations of pragmatic ideas and possibilities but also examples of intelligent, pragmatic *thinking*. As acts of thinking, these works suggest in their various twists and turns, their various urges and inconsistencies, the persistent difficulties but also the extraordinary possibilities and pleasures of what, if we are content to be wisely led by their author, we might consider normal life.

RICHARD FORD AND THE ENDS OF REALISM

ONE

The Lie of Literature and the Work of Mourning

The Sportswriter and *Rock Springs*

Although Richard Ford began reading Emerson's essays in the mid-1970s while teaching at the University of Michigan, Ford's first two novels, *A Piece of My Heart* (1976) and *The Ultimate Good Luck* (1981), show no significant sign of Emersonian influence.[1] It is only with the publication of *The Sportswriter* in 1986 that Ford begins to display the tendencies and concerns that become characteristic of his more mature style, the style that I have tentatively labeled "pragmatic realism." In order to write in this newly pragmatic way, Ford found it necessary to separate himself from previous, less pragmatic ways of writing and thinking, and this is the revisionist task that *The Sportswriter* undertakes. The novel offers itself, in that sense, not only as an example of a new way of writing but also as a justification of it. I begin this first chapter by exploring the specific terms of that justification—I ask what kinds of writing Ford is rejecting in *The Sportswriter* and what form or forms that rejection takes. Having established the nature of the change that is both enacted and argued for in *The Sportswriter*, I then turn, in the remainder of the chapter, to the more difficult issue of cause. I ask *why* Ford changed his style in the early 1980s, and I seek an answer to that question by looking at his personal circumstances during this period, in particular, his response to the death of his mother in December 1981.

Frank Bascombe, *The Sportswriter*'s protagonist, has taken up journalism after abandoning a brief but promising career as a writer of literary fiction. As the novel proceeds, Frank frequently refers back to this career change as a way of commenting on the weaknesses of certain kinds of literature and literary attitudes and in order to note, by way of contrast, his preference for the distinctly different kinds of values and philosophy that he associates with his new way of life. The contrast between these two kinds of writing quickly becomes a contrast between two distinct ways of looking at and thinking about the world, one of which (sportswriting) is down-to-earth but still hopeful, while the other (literature) is sentimental and highfalutin: "If there's another thing that sportswriting teaches you, it is that there are no transcendent themes in life. In all cases things are here and they're over and that has to be enough. The other view is a lie of literature and the liberal arts, which is why I did not succeed as a teacher, and another reason I put my novel away in a drawer and have not taken it out" (*S*, 16).

Frank Bascombe's personal history has obvious links to Richard Ford's. In 1981, after achieving only moderate commercial success with *A Piece of My Heart* and *The Ultimate Good Luck*, Ford gave up writing fiction and took a job with the magazine *Inside Sports*. The following year, however, when *Inside Sports* ceased publication, he returned to fiction, beginning work on *The Sportswriter* in April 1982. In describing this period later in interviews, Ford makes it clear that with *The Sportswriter* he was trying to do something new, that he was "starting off in some totally new direction."[2] A large part of the force of Frank's assault on literature, then, is certainly biographical: it is Ford's way of turning his back on the kind of fiction he had been producing over the previous decade or so and signaling his own effort to do something distinctly different and better. Ford indeed glancingly satirizes his own earlier novels in *The Sportswriter* by having Frank recall *Night Wing*, the novel he wrote as an undergraduate that combines (to inadvertently comic effect) the Southern Gothic and the hard-boiled—precisely the genres Ford himself was working with in *A Piece of My Heart* and *The Ultimate Good Luck*.[3]

Seen within the context of Ford's career more broadly, then, Frank Bascombe's apparent abandonment of writing functions, essentially, as a kind of feint. Although he *claims* to have given up on literature altogether, he is in a very important sense writing the novel that is *The Sportswriter*. Indeed, in suggesting that *The Sportswriter* is not a novel at all, Frank is in one sense claiming that it is *better* than a novel, or at least better than most novels—a point that becomes plain when on arriving in Detroit he notes that his feelings are much more complex than the conventions of literature would allow for:

"This, of course, is the minor but pernicious lie of literature, that at times like these . . . we are any of us altogether *in* an emotion" (*S*, 119). He then goes on to give an adequately complex (implicitly unliterary) description of what those feelings actually are: "What I feel, in truth . . . is, in a word, a *disturbance.* As though I were releasing something venerable but in need of relinquishing. I feel a quickening in my pulse. I feel a strong sense of lurking evil. . . . I feel a conviction that I have no ethics at all and little consistency. I sense the possibility of terrible regret in the brash air. I feel the need suddenly to confide. . . . I feel as literal as I've ever felt. . . . [A]ll these I feel at once" (*S*, 119–20).

As a piece of literary criticism Frank's accusation is not particularly convincing. As any reader of Tolstoy or Virginia Woolf or even Shakespeare will know, some writers are extremely good at rendering the complexity and contradictoriness of their characters' inner lives. But these passages function not as statements of critical fact but rather as disguised expressions of literary preference. When Frank talks about literature in general he actually means a certain form of literature—in other words, Ford is using Frank's shoot-from-the-hip generalizations to suggest certain aesthetic preferences, to make, implicitly, an argument for what good writing should and should not do, and, by doing so, to clear the way for his own mature style. Ford, via Frank, is in this sense simply repeating in an updated context the well-worn novelistic maneuver whereby a new form of realism emerges from the mockery and destruction of earlier, more sentimental or moralistic ways of writing and thinking. Frank's dismissal of literature in toto is a version of the same tactic that we see employed by Flaubert when he mocks Emma Bovary's reading habits in *Madame Bovary* or Henry James when he points out the ludicrousness of Mrs. Penniman's fictionally inspired attempts at matchmaking in *Washington Square.* For all three writers, the novel, as that form is contemporaneously understood, must be swept aside for the novel as *they* understand it (i.e., the truly realist novel) to come into being.

Ford differs, subtly but significantly, from his realist predecessors, however, in his wish to understand this newer form of realism as being characterized by an awareness of complexity and uncertainty as much as by an awareness of the actual and the down-to-earth. Frank's preference for this particular (and particularly pragmatic) kind of writing—the kind that respects both the actual *and* the ungraspable—is suggested most strongly in *The Sportswriter* by his emphasis on the value and importance of mystery. "Mystery," a term that quickly becomes central to the novel, is defined by Frank as "the attractive condition a thing . . . possesses which you know a little about but don't know about completely. It is the twiney promise of unknown things" (*S*, 101). "Mystery," understood thus, becomes contrasted to the dullness, even the despair, of what is fully known and thus contains no possible surprises, what Frank calls the "shabby impingement of facts" and the "indignity of endless explanation" (*S*, 83, 206). The novel's emphasis on this quality of mystery suggests that Frank's mistrust of literary transcendence is not motivated by materialism or essentialism but rather by a kind of down-home version of negative capability in which life is given meaning and purpose only by what is not or cannot be (this important difference is sometimes fudged) properly or fully understood.[4] In order to square this idea with his sportswriter's appreciation of the actual, he coins a contrast between "literalism" and "factualism," the former suggesting an ability to live in and appreciate the here and now, and the latter a dissatisfied yearning after knowledge or sureness (*S*, 132–33). This distinction is reinforced and given a particular literary dimension by Frank's suggestion that writing fiction is usually about trying to discover things that would be far better left unknown—"I do not think . . . it's a good idea to want to know what people are thinking (that would disqualify you as a writer right there, since what else is literature but somebody telling us what somebody else is thinking)" (*S*, 76)—just as literary criticism is usually about explaining things that should be left unexplained. At Berkshire College, where Frank spends an unhappy semester teaching literature, his fellow faculty members are, he tells us, "all anti-mystery types right to the core . . . all expert in the arts of explaining, explicating and dissecting, and by these means promoting permanence. For me that made for the worst kind of despairs" (*S*, 222).

Frank's avowed distrust of literature allows Ford to suggest his dissatisfaction with his own relatively derivative early novels, but it also allows him to subtly position himself within the broader literary culture and to begin to suggest how the pragmatic realism he is developing in *The Sportswriter* differs not only from his own unsuccessful early efforts but also from the more successful work of many of his contemporaries. In December 1982, according to interviews, Ford showed a draft of the first 150 pages of *The Sportswriter* to

Gordon Lish, then senior editor at Knopf and the man, then and since, most closely associated with the "minimalist" trend of the early and mid-1980s. Lish, Ford explains, hated what he saw: "He read about ten pages of it and said, 'You can't write this book. This doesn't work, it's no good. Put it in your drawer and never think about it at all.' These were the kind of broad strokes he generally painted the world in. That was about Christmas-time, 1982, and I had to stop working on [the book] for about seven months because I was so cast down by such a bad opinion."[5] The incident with Lish certainly reinforces the sense that *The Sportswriter* marked a major departure for Ford himself, but it also opens up the possibility that in writing in this new way Ford was going against not only his own earlier practices but also a larger set of contemporary literary tendencies—it raises, in other words, the interesting but far from straightforward question of Ford's relationship to the kind of "minimalist" neorealism associated with Lish and Raymond Carver and that, following the publication of Carver's critically acclaimed (and very heavily Lish-influenced) *What We Talk About When We Talk About Love* in 1981, was very much in the air when Ford set to work on his third novel.[6]

The conventional literary history of this period connects Ford to this movement, since he was good friends with Carver, Tobias Wolff, and Anne Beattie (all of whom were linked with the "new" realism) and was featured as one of Bill Buford's American "dirty realists" in the influential issues of *Granta* published in 1983 and 1986. Even a casual reading of *The Sportswriter* alongside *What We Talk About When We Talk About Love* reveals, however, huge differences between the two works in both style and theme. By 1982 Ford was turning away from the view of the world that associated "darkness with drama" and toward a more nuanced and ultimately more optimistic vision. He made this clear in a 1996 interview during which he remembered, "I had begun, out of youthful ignorance and ardor, to associate darkness—emotional, spiritual, moral darkness—with high drama. . . . But by the time 1982 rolled around, I realised I could no longer sustain identifying darkness with drama. I just sort of ground to a halt."[7] He also explicitly wrote this change of mind into *The Sportswriter* in the form of Frank's reservations about his own fiction: "What I did as I began writing *Tangier* . . . was become more and more grave. . . . My characters generally embodied the attitude that life is always going to be a damn nasty and probably baffling business, but somebody has to go slogging through it. This, of course, can eventually lead to terrible cynicism, since I knew life wasn't like that at all" (*S*, 46–47).

While Ford is certainly not directly criticizing Carver, Lish, or the other writers associated with literary minimalism in *The Sportswriter*, he is, I think, signaling the differences between his work and theirs. This, for example, is Frank's self-deprecating description of the stories in his first and only collection, *Blue Autumn*: "Most of them were set in places like remote hunting camps on Canadian lakes, or in the suburbs, or Arizona or Vermont, places I had never been, and many of them ended with men staring out snowy windows in New England boarding schools or with somebody driving fast down a dark dirt road, or banging his hand into a wall, or telling someone else he could never *really* love his wife, and bringing on hard emptinesses. They also seemed to depend on silence a lot" (*S*, 46). While the locations of these fictional fictions recall Tobias Wolff, another so-called dirty realist, the emphasis on silence is distinctly Carveresque, since, as the term "minimalism" suggests, Carver's fiction and that of other writers associated with the "school" was distinguished as much for what it left out as for what it included. Michael Wood's laudatory front-page review of *What We Talk About When We Talk About Love* in the *New York Times Book Review* in April 1981, for example, was typically titled "Stories Full of Edges and Silences" and concluded with the observation that "in Mr. Carver's silences, a good deal of the unsayable gets said." Although Ford argued in a 1986 interview that Carver's stories aren't always as silent as they seem and consequently aren't as different from his own work as they might at first appear,[8] he also in the important 1983 essay "The Three Kings: Faulkner, Hemingway, Fitzgerald" mounted a quite detailed and sustained attack on literary reticence (or showing rather than telling) as exemplified in the work of Hemingway, its most famous exemplar, whom Ford calls the "great-taker-outer." Although Ford remembers admiring Hemingway's stories when he first read them, he also remembers feeling from the very beginning that they were flawed or limited. Hemingway, he argues, says too little and "made too much of silences."

Although "The Three Kings," which was commissioned and published by *Harper's*, purports to be about literary influence, it tells us at least as much about Ford's thinking in 1983, when he was thirty-nine years old and working on *The Sportswriter*, as it does about his earlier formative experiences. The differences between Hemingway and Faulkner in this essay stand in, in rough but important ways, for the differences between the old style of writing Ford was trying to move away from in the early eighties and the new style he was trying to adopt. *The Sportswriter*'s crucial quality of mystery is, in particular, central to the contrast Ford is making between Hemingway and Faulkner. While Hemingway creates a sense of mystery by keeping quiet, Ford tells us, Faulkner creates it by writing, in some important sense, too much.[9] The difference is one of tone, style, and technique but also, Ford makes clear, of emotional and psychological development. To rely on silence, Ford insists, is to employ a "young man's aesthetic" designed primarily to impress other young men. It is, in other words, a very clear sign of immaturity:

> To me, Hemingway kept secrets rather than discovered them. He held the overcomplex world too much at arm's length either because he wouldn't on principle or couldn't say more. And for that reason I distrusted him. He valued accuracy and precision over truth, and for that reason, despite his effects, he seemed a specialist in what he himself called "minor passions." Even today, when I am always surprised at how much broader a writer he is than I remember, he still seems a high school team captain with codes, a man who peaked too early and never went on to greater, harder feats.[10]

In the same section of the 1986 interview in which he downplayed Carver's silences, Ford also sidestepped the suggestion that *The Sportswriter*'s loquacious and introspective style goes "against the grain of contemporary American fiction" by pointing out that at the same time as he was writing the novel he was also working on a book of short stories set in Montana that "are nothing like it."[11] Ford's remarks in this interview may obscure as much as they illuminate, but reading *Rock Springs*, his 1987 short story collection, in light of *The Sportswriter*, is indeed an interesting and disconcerting experience. One notices not only that the two works are stylistically and thematically quite distinct (as he admits they are) but also that many of the stories seem to rehearse the same minimalist and Hemingwayesque tendencies that both Frank and Ford condemn as weaknesses in their own early work. The kind of "writerly serious[ness]" that Frank has escaped from by giving up fiction and that Ford attempted to escape from by beginning *The Sportswriter* is, in particular, a frequent characteristic of *Rock Springs.* These are stories preoccupied with the male experience of abandonment and betrayal, or at least with the ever-present fear of abandonment and betrayal, and the all-male protagonists are almost to a man (or boy) laconic and emotionally inarticulate. John Edgar Wideman's 1987 review of *Rock Springs* in the *New York Times* accurately noted that "with Mr. Ford's characters we are adrift in a world where possibilities seem to be closing down, a region of moral defeat and exhaustion whose inhabitants are losing or have lost or are barely clinging to a sense of purpose, dignity."

Given that *Rock Springs* was published so soon after *The Sportswriter* and most of the stories were written at the same time as Ford was working on the novel, we might justifiably wonder why Ford was writing in two such distinctly different and opposing ways during the same period. What explains his unembarrassed use in *Rock Springs* of the very style that in *The Sportswriter* he was trying so clearly to diminish and move away from? Ford's own response when questioned on this issue is that such duality is normal, even natural, but we may suspect that there is at least a little more to it than that.[12] If we remember that in "The Three Kings" Ford strongly associated the move from Hemingwayesque silence to Faulknerian loquaciousness with the process of male maturation, then the strange persistence of this earlier, more clearly Hemingwayesque style may certainly be seen as a clue that the stylistic tensions apparent in Ford's writing in the early and mid-1980s had some kind of significant psychological corollary.

The early and mid-1980s were indeed an emotionally charged and clearly transitional period in Richard Ford's life. He has described 1981 in particular as a year of "extreme personal heartache and stress."[13] His living and working arrangements were unsettled, and, most importantly, his mother's breast cancer, which had been in remission, had returned. In "My Mother in Memory," a short memoir published in *Harper's* in 1987, he remembers the months leading up to her death in December that year as "an awful time . . . when life felt ruined, futureless, edging towards disappointments."[14] Ford's reinvention of himself as a writer from 1982 onward occurs very clearly, then, in the context of the painful loss of his mother—a loss that is certainly figured or remembered in *The Sportswriter* in the form of Frank's dead son, Ralph. Although Ralph is mentioned infrequently, his death motivates the whole novel, which begins at his graveside on what would have been his thirteenth birthday and ends with Frank declaring that his mourning for his son is finally ended. That Ralph's death stands in large part for the death of Ford's mother is made clear in a 1986 interview in which the interviewer, Kay Bonetti, having noted the way Ford's work frequently returns to the experience of loss, asks where that concern comes from, and Ford replies: "Lately in the last four or five years, I think probably fairly directly from my mother, whom I love very much and miss now that she's gone."[15] Both *The Sportswriter* and *Rock Springs* are in that sense, I want to suggest, works that emerge from and to some extent dramatize the process of mourning. We must now turn to that complex and variegated process to help explain the particular and peculiar relationship between these two works.

What such an analysis suggests, when taken together with the arguments I have already made, is the complex and overdetermined nature of Ford's movement in the mid-1980s into the mature style that I have called "pragmatic realism." On the one hand, in producing *The Sportswriter*, Ford simply rejected the methods and presuppositions of his own earlier work and of the work of the contemporary minimalist school more generally. At the same time, however, as I will now attempt to show, he also associated those methods with a particular attitude toward loss and thus by extension with a particular phase of his own mourning and maturational processes. Ford's literary and stylistic development thus became overlaid and entangled, in ways that may have been psychologically inevitable but are, nonetheless, surprising and interesting to consider, with his responses to his mother's death. As a result, the successful end of mourning announced by Frank Bascombe (in relation to Ralph) in the last few pages of *The Sportswriter* became for Ford, implicitly but importantly, synonymous with the beginning of a new, more optimistic, and finally more successful way of writing—an emotional and literary coincidence that is subtly signaled by Frank's declaration:

> My heart still beats, though not, in truth, exactly as it did before.
> My voice is as strong and plausible as I can ever remember it. (*S*, 371)

In his famous essay of 1917, "Mourning and Melancholia," Freud describes the work of mourning as being gradual and as consisting of two distinct elements: first, the phase of "reality testing," that is, the slow recognition, experienced through a series of engagements with memories, places, and so on, connected to the dead person, that the lost object really is lost; and second, the decision, given that that is indeed the case, to go on living: "Each single one of the memories and situations of expectancy which demonstrate the libido's attachment to the lost object is met by the verdict of reality that the object no longer exists; and the ego, confronted as it were with the question whether it shall share this fate, is persuaded by the sum of the narcissistic satisfactions it derives from being alive to sever its attachment to the object that has been abolished."[16] This two-fold structure, although no doubt schematic, offers a suggestive way to begin reading the differences between *Rock Springs* and *The Sportswriter*. Whereas *The Sportswriter*, with its emphasis on the power and importance of conventionality, is devoted quite explicitly to the mourner's effort to return to normal life by reconnecting to a substitute love object, *Rock Springs*, in contrast, is given over almost completely to the more primitive and painful task of learning and then relearning the fact that the mother is lost and will never return.[17] The stylistic contradictions between *Rock Springs* and *The Sportswriter* express in this way two equally necessary but also contradictory elements of mourning: the confusion and agony of loss *and* the desire to recover from it and return to something like normality.

The strongest piece of evidence linking *Rock Springs* to the death of Ford's mother is the title story, which opens the collection. The story begins: "Edna and I had started down from Kalispell, heading for Tampa St. Pete." Since Edna is the name of Ford's mother and the story was written in New York in February 1981, after her cancer had returned and ten months before her death, it seems highly likely that Ford, whether consciously or unconsciously, was writing about his mother and the potential loss of his mother through the character of Edna.[18] This likelihood is reinforced by the fact that the story pivots on Edna's decision to leave Earl (the story's protagonist and Edna's boyfriend), a decision that leaves him angry and "in shock." Discussing the story in an interview in 1986, Ford identified his own voice explicitly with Earl's and also picked out Edna's final words to Earl as the story's key moment: "When Edna says to Earl, 'It's not a matter of not loving you,' that's everything to me."[19] The story's ending becomes a way, in other words, for Ford to both represent the loss of his mother and reassure himself that that loss (when it comes) will not amount to a deliberate emotional rejection. The desire for such reassurance, while understandable in the context of a failed love affair, suggests in the context of mourning the paranoid fear that, in the words of Melanie Klein, "by dying the loved one was seeking to inflict punishment and deprivation upon him [the mourner]."[20] Although the appearance of such a fear and of the resentment or even hatred that it may provoke is not unusual, according to Klein, it does indicate that the process of mourning still has some way to go.

Elsewhere in *Rock Springs*, notably in the three coming-of-age stories ("Great Falls," "Optimists," and "Communist"), we see the painful departure of the mother replayed rather more literally. All three stories feature male teenage protagonists who experience the collapse of their family or substitute family, and all three end with emotionally charged, subtly sexualized, and therefore psychologically unsatisfactory farewell encounters between mother and son. At the end of "Great Falls," for example, the son leaves school in the middle of the day to meet his mother in a motel room, where she asks him for "a nice compliment," while in "Communist" the mother, after getting her son out of bed to listen to the geese flying overhead, asks him whether he thinks she's still "very feminine." The obviously, if subtly, Oedipal nature of these encounters serves to remind us of the extent to which mourning (especially the mourning of the dead mother) echoes the earlier Oedipal process of separation and substitution, but it also has the effect of emphasizing the extreme difficulty, almost the impossibility, of the position that the son as mourner is placed in. In the classical Oedipal situation, the mother-child relationship is severed by the father, who threatens castration but also offers an alternative model of being; in Ford's later replayings, however, the father figure is absent, and therefore the only alternative to the mother's impossible love (impossible within the Oedipal context because incestuous, and impossible within the context of mourning because the mother is in fact dead) is the complete absence of love. The seriousness of this psychological impasse is made clear in "Communist" by Les's internal response to his mother's question ("Do you think I'm still very feminine?"): "And I felt the way you feel when you are on a trestle all alone and the train is coming and you know you have to decide. And I said 'Yes, I do.' Because that was the truth. And I tried to think of something else then and did not hear what my mother said after that" (*RS*, 235). The image of standing on the trestle and knowing the train is approaching suggests the calamitous possibility that although the mother cannot or should not any longer be loved, no substitute love object exists, and therefore the work of detaching oneself from the mother becomes a kind of emotional suicide. The nihilistic ending of "Great Falls" suggests much the same thing. After listing a number of questions about the behavior of his parents on the night his mother's extramarital affair was discovered, Jackie, the protagonist, concludes: "But I have never known the answer to these questions, have never asked anyone their answers. Though possibly it—the answer—is simple: it is just low-life, some coldness in us all, some helplessness which causes us to misunderstand life when it is pure and plain, makes our existence seem like a border between two nothings and makes us no more or less than animals who meet on the road—watchful, unforgiving, without patience or desire" (*RS*, 49).

If "Great Falls," "Optimists," and "Communist" are all stories that indirectly figure or dramatize the process of mourning the dead mother, then we can say that the mourning they dramatize is clearly incomplete or unsuccessful, since all three end with a sense of continuing, perhaps continual loss. Other stories in the collection, however, offer something closer to resolution in the orthodox Freudian sense.

In "Fireworks" the protagonist, Eddie Starling, is described by his wife as a "momma's boy" and seems through most of the story to be suffering a kind of psychic and emotional immaturity that is linked to his inability to detach himself from his mother, who is now dead, and take on an adult role. To underline this point, Starling remembers in gruesome detail the abortion performed on his first wife fifteen years earlier and paid for by his mother, and, linked to that memory, he receives a mysterious collect call from a young man who is in trouble and who claims to be his son. Starling refuses the call ("No dads here") but then almost immediately thinks "he should've accepted the charges, said a word of consolation, or given some advice since the kid seemed at wit's end" (*RS*, 201). Starling cannot offer adequate parental consolation, we are surely expected to conclude, because he still requires it himself—he is still, at thirty-nine, a kind of child. He tells us he is in as much trouble as the boy who called and wishes disconsolately that his mother was still alive so he could ask her for assistance (*RS*, 204).

Starling's emotional stuntedness and lack of authority are reinforced by the fact that he has recently lost his job and is now living in a second-rate neighborhood and surviving on his wife's wages as a bartender. The story ends, however, with a moment of hope that is clearly attached to a larger, unspoken process of mourning and resolution. While driving home, Eddie and his wife, Lois, remember how Eddie's mother had enjoyed fireworks and in particular had liked to hold the "little teenies" in her hands as they went off. In the story's final paragraph, Lois takes the deceased mother's place by getting out of the car and dancing around in front of Eddie while holding sparklers in the same way his mother used to.

> Then Lois closed the door and danced out before the car into the rain with the sparklers, waving her arms round in the air, smiling widely and making swirls and patterns and star-falls for him that were brilliant and illuminated the night and the bright rain and the little dark house behind her and, for a moment, caught the world and stopped it, as though something sudden and perfect had come to earth in a furious glowing for him and for him alone—Eddie Starling—and only he could watch and listen. And only he would be there, waiting, when the light was finally gone. (*RS*, 214)

From the Freudian point of view, Lois is clearly offering herself here as a substitute love object, and the story is thus at least holding out the possibility that Eddie will finally be able to detach himself from his mother and complete the work of mourning. This possibility is strongly reinforced by the symbolism of the fireworks. As Peter M. Sacks's work on the English poetic elegy makes plain, natural light in the form of fire, stars, or the sun is a standard consolatory symbol that has been used since antiquity to suggest the triumph of the eternal over the forces of death. Sacks even goes so far as to note in relation to Thomas Hardy's elegy for Swinburne, "A Singer Asleep," that "little could be more conventional than to transform the dead into a source of natural light."[21] Clearly, in "Fireworks" this ancient mythic consolation is tinged with a measure of modern secular doubt—if the world and time can temporarily be stopped, they will eventually begin again, the light will eventually go out, and Eddie will be left alone. Nevertheless, the moment suggests the possibility of a consolation that, if not permanent, is certainly real.

A similar set of images is brought into play at the conclusion of "Empire," which ends with Vic Sims, the protagonist, lying down next to his wife, Marge, in the sleeping compartment of a train while the prairie outside is burning: “Outside on the cold air, flames moved and divided and swarmed the sky. And Sims felt all alone in a wide empire, removed and afloat, calmed, as if life was far away now, as if blackness was all around, as if stars held the only light” (*RS*, 148). Earlier, while Marge was sleeping, Sims had sex with another woman, a female soldier, Sergeant Benton, whom he met in the parlor car. This act of adultery in turn recalls an incident a year before when Sims slept with Cleo, the sister of a neighbor, while Marge was in the hospital with what Sims believed was terminal cancer. It is clear enough, then, that Sims’s sexual escapades are linked to an awareness and a fear of death. Recalling Klein, we might suggest they are in part acts of vengeance born of the paranoid belief that the loved one’s death is a deliberate withdrawal of affection. Feelings of hatred or animosity toward the deceased that become linked in turn to feelings of guilt and self-hatred are typical features of more complex mourning processes. Such convoluted and unconscious defense mechanisms are surely present when, just after he has had sex with Cleo, Sims dreams that he has been found hanged but that Marge has survived her cancer: “In his dream Sims had hanged himself from a tall pine-tree limb in a forest somewhere. . . . Yet, even though he was dead and hanging from a new rope with birds perched on top of his head, Marge was somehow still alive and in her hospital room, smiling out of a sunny window, looking better than she had in weeks” (*RS*, 131–32). Neither Sims’s dream life nor his sexual behavior, past and present, suggests that he has yet come to terms with his fear of Marge’s death or that the larger process of maternal mourning that the story figures is close to being resolved. The fire that rages outside their train at the story’s end is an image at best of careless natural destruction and at worst of the kind of moral retribution frequently associated within Christian iconography with images of burning. Within this disturbing context, the final image of the stars offers only a slight and distant sense of consolation. That Ford reaches for it at all, however, is suggestive, since it indicates the desire, more fully realized and thought through in *The Sportswriter*, to go beyond the repeated recognition and absorption of loss and to find a way to bring the mourning process to an end.

As Peter Sacks makes plain, the normal, long-established, elegiac model achieves resolution by invoking or discovering a convincing image of the eternal either in the work of art itself or in other related mythic or religious symbols. If most of the stories of *Rock Springs* fail to achieve any kind of consolation, this failure is signaled by the general absence of such symbols within them and also, stylistically, by the stories' insistent artlessness.[22] Instead of the metaphorical plenitude and lyrical ambition of *The Sportswriter*, the writing in *Rock Springs* is generally flat and straightforward (minimalist, one might even suggest), rising and taking on weight only at the moments when it devotes itself to the concrete particularities of the characters' working lives. (The brief exceptions are the passages from "Fireworks" and "Empire" that I have quoted, in which the imagery of light is accompanied by a distinct shift of stylistic register.) In *The Sportswriter*, in contrast, Ford engages much more fully with the consolatory possibilities of both style and symbolism.[23] The terms of this engagement, however, are far from straightforward. As we have already seen in Frank's complex, equivocating relationship to literature, Ford must first reject certain inherited models before he can then go on to invent his own truer or more "original" versions of them. This need for originality even in the face of something so apparently permanent and unoriginal as death is, according again to Sacks, a characteristic quality of American writing and brings with it a particular set of problems:

> One of the striking, but not surprising, differences between the English elegy and the American is the latter's loss, rejection, or radically transformative borrowing of the traditional myths and contexts of the genre. Partly because of obvious geographical and ideological differences, but also because of a strong compulsion towards originality and privacy, American elegists could not easily situate their poems in the familiar pastoral settings or even within the familiar ritual procedures of the genre. American elegists have had not only to reinvent the forms (if not the functions) of elegiac mythology but also to establish their own literal and figurative settings.[24]

In his adoption of American suburbia in general and Haddam, New Jersey, in particular as a symbol of pastoral simplicity and continuity, Ford is doing precisely the kind of revisionist work that Sacks is talking about here.[25] As a consolatory symbol, Haddam stands in contrast to the cluster of Christian ideas and symbols that Ford invokes but also eventually dismisses. Although the novel's Easter-time setting seems to suggest that Ford is using the inherited symbols of Christianity to think through the experience of loss and mourning, these ideas and symbols ultimately serve as a foil for Ford's more secular and pragmatic alternative. The novel's ultimate Christian symbol, in this sense, is the extraordinarily garish near-life-size figure of Christ on the cross that is attached to the front of the Arcenaults' house on the day of Frank's calamitous visit: "Jesus in his suburban agony. Bloody eyes. Flimsy body. Feet already beginning to sag and give up the ghost" (*S*, 243). The point of this is not to suggest the moral failures of the suburbs by ironic contrast to the integrity or timelessness of Christ's message but rather to suggest the irrelevance or worse of such mythology within the contemporary American context. When Frank notices the statue again while standing in the yard during his climactic argument with Vicki, his girlfriend, the point is clearly and crudely made: "I cast a wintery eye at Lynette's spurious beigey Jesus nailed to the siding. He makes life a perfect misery for as many as he can, then never takes the heat. He should try resurrection in today's complex world. He'd fall right off His cross on His ass" (*S*, 294). Ford uses Christianity here and more generally in much the same way as he uses "literature" earlier in the novel: they both stand for the inherited ways of thinking about and responding to loss, ways that must be cleared away before newer and better alternatives can be offered. In interviews Ford has insisted vigorously that *The Sportswriter* is in no sense a Christian novel and has used the term "secular redemption" to describe the difference between the hope he is attempting to offer in *The Sportswriter* and the kind that is traditionally offered by Christianity. While this term is useful, it is also broad—we might well ask what such secular redemption might look and feel like and how it can be lived. Sacks's point that American writers tend to reinvent the *forms* but not the function of elegiac mythology is relevant here. Ford is certainly not giving up on consolation—the novel indeed ends with Frank's declaration that his mourning period for his son Ralph is now over—but he is offering a new and particular version of it.

A large part of this newness is Ford's decision to offer, without irony, the New Jersey suburbs and the ways of life associated with it as a believable version of American pastoral.[26] The novel makes this point again and again both in Frank's loving and lyrical descriptions of the suburban landscape through which he moves and, more directly, in passages such as the following, where renting a car becomes a kind of modern-day fertility rite: "There is nothing quite like the first moments inside a big, strapping fleet-clean LTD or Montego—mileage checked, tank full, seat adjusted, the heavy door closed tight, the stirring 'new' smell in your nostrils—the confidence that here is a car better even than the one you own (and even better than that, since you only have to ask for another one if this one craps out). To me, there is no feeling of freedom-within-sensible-limits quite like that. New today. New tomorrow. Eternal renewal on a manageable scale" (*S*, 148). There can be no doubt that in passages like this Ford is using, or trying to use, the suburbs as a symbol of consolation in the same way that poets since antiquity have used flowers, birds, stars, the sun, and so on. But this substitution, although energetically and convincingly asserted, still appears shaky at times. Ford's revisionist symbolism, perhaps because it is more original and idiosyncratic, also seems sometimes as weak as the inherited symbols it has replaced—an effort of individual will that may easily fail. This feeling comes to the fore in the final movement of the novel following Walter Luckett's suicide. When Frank reenters Haddam after learning of Walter's death, he finds the town unable to support the weight of symbolic meanings he has previously placed upon it. The town is unable to serve a consolatory function because it is unable to resist or transcend death. Instead of the "swimming pool odor I trust," the town has a "crusty death's smell" (*S*, 314), and when Frank sees a family cheerfully cycling home from their "Danish-modern Unitarian hug-a-friend church" he bursts into a denunciation of the very values he has spent much of the novel promoting: "But they are wrong, wrong, these Jamiesons. I should tell them. Life-forever is a lie of the suburbs—its worst lie—and a fact worth knowing before you get caught in its fragrant silly dream" (*S*, 319).

Peter Sacks has pointed out that the American elegists' reluctance to employ traditional figures of consolation—their desire instead for individuation and originality—puts them in a vulnerable position and may make them "especially susceptible to the appeal, and not merely the threat, of death."[27] This is the case for Whitman, for example, in "When Lilacs Last in the Dooryard Bloomed," when his efforts to metaphorically "deck" Lincoln's coffin fail, and the poem turns into a carol in praise of death. This, or something very like it, seems also to be the case for Frank Bascombe when, after the apparent failure of his self-fashioned suburban mythology, he is left alone in a state "beyond all hopes," a state that seems from the way in which he describes it to be quite similar to actually being dead: "Just to slide away like a whisper down the wind is no small freedom, and if we're lucky enough to win such a setting-free, even if it's bad events that cause it, we should use it, for it is the only naturally occurring consolation that comes to us, sole and sovereign, without props or the forbearance of others" (*S*, 339). This state *seems* death-like because what is being described is a loss of self; yet the section as a whole makes clear that such a loss is to be understood not as an endpoint or a fantasy of suicide but as a probably necessary and certainly welcome transition from one identity or way of thinking to another. If one system of consolation has failed, Frank is suggesting, then another, better one is likely to appear soon enough. In order to figure this state of transition, Ford himself employs the image of invisibility—a literary trope whose complex provenance includes, most obviously, the work of H. G. Wells and Claude Rains but also (and surely more importantly for Ford) Emerson's Coleridgean notions of transparency and Ralph Ellison's racialized revision of that metaphor in his seminal 1952 novel *Invisible Man*:

> Walter would say that I have become neither the seer nor the thing seen—as invisible as Claude Rains in the movie, though I have no enemies to get back at, no debts to pay off. Invisibility in truth is not so bad. We should all try to know it better, use it to our advantage the way Claude Rains didn't, since at one time or another—like it or not—we all become invisible, loosed from body and duty, left to drift on the night breeze, to do as we will, to cast about for what we would like to be when we next occur. That, let me promise you is not an empty moment. And further yet from real regret. (*S*, 339)

Lee Rust Brown has argued that transparency in Emerson functions as "an allegory of mental life as a whole," meaning that the metaphor of transparency (as most famously employed in the "transparent eyeball" passage in *Nature*) stands for the ability of the self to dissolve and then reassemble in a new and different form, to change creatively, in other words, in response to a changing experience.[28] This is certainly the sense in which Ford is using the metaphor of invisibility in *The Sportswriter*—Frank's self at this point in the novel may have lost its specificity, may have become blurred and boundaryless, but this is understood not as a reason for anxiety but rather as a refreshing prelude to him being remade in some new and better form. Although the metaphor is at root Romantic and Emersonian, as Brown makes clear, Frank's association of invisibility with a particular racial experience suggests that Ford is drawing his inspiration most directly from Ralph Waldo Ellison—Emerson's namesake and pragmatic successor—more than from Emerson himself. Shortly after the passage quoted above, Frank thinks of visiting his African lodger, Bosobolo, to "talk to him about invisibility" but then decides that "a true African would know less than one of our local Negroes, and I would end up explaining a lot to start with" (*S*, 340). In connecting Frank to Ellison or to Emerson via Ellison, Ford is clearly attaching his protagonist and himself to a particularly American line of liberal and pragmatic thought that emphasizes fluidity and self-creation over identity and sureness.[29] Invisibility in Ellison's famous epilogue to *Invisible Man* is connected to possibility, specifically, the democratic possibility promised although not yet delivered by the founding of the United States. To be invisible is to have escaped any fixed role or definition and thus to be not dead, alienated, or unmanned but potentially, at least, free: "I assign myself no rank or any limit. . . . [M]y world has become one of infinite possibilities."[30]

Since invisibility is a rich and storied symbol, and Ellison is a highly allusive and deeply American writer who self-consciously absorbed and revised the work of his nineteenth- and twentieth-century predecessors from Emerson to Faulkner, one useful way of understanding this gesture is to see it as Ford's way of placing himself within a particular literary *community*—a community that then exerts a consoling power first because it includes other people (Frank is symbolically no longer alone, even if literally he is) and second because as an ongoing intellectual tradition it transcends the death of the individual.[31] Ellison and his progenitors live on in their work and in the minds of their readers in the same way that traditional elegists imagine that they themselves as poets, like the dead they remember, will in some sense live on in their poem. What is both theorized *and* enacted then in this key passage is the transition from one consolatory metaphor or group of metaphors to another. The allusion to Ellison signals that Ford is associating himself with pragmatic values of fluidity and originality, while Frank's taking on of invisibility signals that he, as a character, has abandoned one way of thinking and is ready to find a new one. I say *group* of metaphors here because in invoking so plainly his literary predecessors Ford is signaling a shift away from the suburban pastoral but also from the antiliterary stance of the earlier sections of the novel. Frank is still seeking connection and community as an antidote to loss and regret, but he is seeking and finding it now within the implicit and timeless community of American writing rather than within the more concrete but temporarily unavailable satisfactions of home and marriage. It is useful to recall here Ford's remarks on Faulkner in "The Three Kings," particularly his suggestion that at a certain point Faulkner's style takes on a life of its own and begets its own distinct and separate genealogy:

> Faulkner dazzled me, of course, as his writing inevitably will. But being from where he was from, I was already acquainted with the way the white man's peculiar experience in that particular locale over time begot the need to tell; to rehearse, explain, twist, revise, and alibi life clear out of its own weirdness and paradox and eventually into a kind of fulgent, cumulative and acceptable sense. Begot, in fact, so much larruping and fabricating that language somehow became paramount for its own sake (a fresh idea to me) and in turn begot its own irony, its own humors, and genealogy and provenance.[32]

What Ford refers to in that essay as the "consolations" of literary style include not only its ability to please and charm the reader's ear but also, one might say, its ability to create and participate in its own particular history, to invoke, memorialize, and revise the writers of the past.

That Ford, by the end of *The Sportswriter*, is committed to a model of consolation that is grounded not in a group of fixed or inherited symbols (whether old or new) but rather in an ongoing, historically inflected process of symbolization or metaphor making is underlined by Frank's movement out of the condition of invisibility. After driving aimlessly around Haddam, he finds himself drawn to the railroad station, where the last train from Philadelphia is just pulling in. He stops to watch the passengers disembark:

> I enjoy this closeness to trains and the great moment they exude, their implacable hissing noise and purpose. I read somewhere it is psychologically beneficial to stand near things greater and more powerful than you yourself, so as to dwarf yourself (and your piddlyass bothers) by

> comparison. To do so, the writer said, released the spirit from its everyday moorings, and accounted for why Montanans and Sherpas who live near daunting mountains, aren't much at complaining or nettlesome introspection. . . . All alone now beside the humming train cars, I actually do feel my moorings slacken, and I will say it again, perhaps for the last time: there is mystery everywhere, even in a vulgar, urine-scented, suburban depot such as this. (*S*, 342)

The railroad, as Leo Marx made plain in 1964, is one of the most venerable and important of American literary symbols, and in invoking it here as part of Frank's turning away from the revisionist pastoralism of Haddam, Ford is recapitulating the movement in nineteenth-century American writing from the pastoral to the technological sublime.[33] Mystery, it seems, is an eminently moveable concept for Frank—an Emersonian principle that Frank takes even further by getting on the train himself and going to New York, a city that he has previously disliked but that when he arrives he immediately sees in a completely different way: "Here, out on Seventh and 34th, I feel an unaccustomed lankness, a post-coital Midwestern caress to things—the always dusky air still high and hollowish, streets alive with the girdering wheels of hungry traffic that pours past me and quickly vanishes" (*S*, 352). This rapid abandonment of old symbols and taking up of new ones may seem frivolous, inconsistent, or even contradictory; there is certainly no place for it in Freud's classic account, which imagines successful mourning involving a simple, if hard-won, substitution of a new love object for what has been lost. Yet for Ford, as for Emerson, such permanence is a fantasy, and what may seem like inconsistency is actually an embrace of life: "Life is a series of surprises. We do not guess today the mood, the pleasure, the power of tomorrow."[34] The end of mourning that Frank announces at the end of the novel is thus not really an end so much as it is the beginning or rebeginning of a process of loss and self-recovery that grief has interrupted or distorted. As Emerson's famous account of grief in "Experience" suggests, the real problem with mourning is that it doesn't take you anywhere different or teach you anything new: "I grieve that grief can teach me nothing, nor carry me one step into real nature."[35] It is in that sense that grief is the opposite of life, which is always new and educational whether we like it or not, and in that sense also, for Ford, that it is the opposite of writing or style, which, as the allusiveness of *The Sportswriter* and the biblical "begettings" that he uses to describe Faulkner's style suggest, is itself inherently generative and fertile.

Close to the very end of the novel, Frank notes archly that "things occur differently to me now, just as they might to a character at the end of a good short story. I have different words for what I see and anticipate, even different sorts of thoughts and reactions; more mature ones, ones that seem to really count" (*S*, 369–70). This is Ford's final laconic play on the literariness or unliterariness of the kind of realism he is attempting. In another context it might be tempting to read such a passage as playfully postmodern, a sly reminder that Frank is just a character in a novel and that fiction is just a particular way of arranging words on a page, but that is surely not Ford's point. Finding new words, new ways of describing one's situation, is the form change actually takes, Ford suggests, but, as all three novels in the Bascombe trilogy make clear, such change is rarely if ever a matter solely of writerly power or of linguistic slippage. It occurs more often than not as a response to the crude, explosive incursions of fact (e.g., the death of Ralph or the suicide of Walter Luckett), which Frank would prefer to avoid or transcend but sometimes can't. Ford's embrace in *The Sportswriter* of literariness or metaphor making as a means of escape from grief remains in this sense carefully measured, its celebratoriness restrained by a realist's persistent, if variable, sense of the mournful weight of the nonliterary, of the effects of a world unshaped and untamed by language.

TWO

Independence Day and the Limits of Pragmatism

When Frank declares at the end of *The Sportswriter* that his mourning for his son Ralph is finally over, he means, as I have just suggested, not so much that he has discovered, in Freudian terms, an effective symbolic substitute for his dead son but, rather more pragmatically, that he has embraced the ongoing process of substitution or metaphor making as a consoling and optimistic way of moving forward into the future. This form of emotional settlement is clearly still in place at the beginning of *Independence Day*, which is by some distance the most overtly Emersonian and pragmatic of the three Bascombe novels. Through much of *Independence Day* Frank appears, often in striking contrast to those around him, to be able to shake off the various mistakes, regrets, and traumas of the past and to be able, as a result, to look forward in an optimistic but unsentimental way to the possibilities of the future. This outlook finds its practical equivalent in Frank's new profession of realtor, an occupation that in *The Lay of the Land* he suggestively compares to that of the novelist: "Realtors share a basic industry with novelists, who make up importance from life-run-rampant just by choosing, changing and telling. Realtors make importance by selling, which is better-paying than the novelist's deal and probably not as hard to do well" (*LL*, 84). Much of the drama of the novel, especially in its early stages, emerges from the collision of Frank's pragmatic viewpoint with the much less pragmatic, and therefore much more backward-looking and mournful, perspectives of those around him. Frank is confronted, in particular, by the maddening intransigence of his fifteen-year-old son, Paul, and of Joe and Phyllis Markham, a couple who wish to buy a house in Haddam but who are still unable, after forty-eight viewings, to find one that suits their requirements. It is Frank's self-imposed task, we soon realize, to release both Paul and the Markhams from the rigidities of their own psychic histories and thus to make them in the broadest sense free.

Paul Bascombe, we are told, is "waging a complex but losing struggle to forget certain things" (*ID*, 13). He is held captive by "memory, history, bad events he struggles with, can't control, but feels he should" (*ID*, 16). Specifically, he has not been able to come to terms with his brother's death and his parents' subsequent divorce, a twin trauma that he simultaneously engages with and avoids by obsessing on the contemporaneous death of the family dog, Mr. Toby: "Now he thinks about Mr. Toby 'a lot' (possibly constantly), thinks that Mr. Toby should be alive still and we should have him—and by extension, of course, that his poor brother, Ralph, who died of Reyes, should also be alive (as he surely should) and we should all still be we" (*ID*, 14).

At first glance, the Markhams' problem seems rather different, but actually it has a similar root. The Markhams, in particular Joe, are psychologically paralyzed by an awareness of their own previous errors of judgment. They cannot move on because they cannot be sure they will not simply repeat the mistakes of the past: "Joe, I'm sure, has been brooding all over again this morning about his whopper miscues—miscues about marriage, divorce, remarriage. . . . All this is a natural part of the aging process, in which you find yourself with less to do and more opportunities to eat your guts out regretting everything you *have* done. But Joe doesn't want to make another whopper, since one more big one might just send him to the bottom" (*ID*, 54). The Markhams' false solution to this dilemma is to seek an ideal—a house so obviously perfect that it could not possibly be wrong. But as Frank makes clear, such ideal houses, and by pragmatic extension ideals in general, do not exist: "Unhappily the Markhams, out of ignorance and pig-headedness, have failed to intuit the one Gnostic truth of real estate . . . that people never find or buy the house they say they want. . . . Why should you only get what you think you want, or be limited by what you can simply plan on? Life's never like that, and if you're smart you'll decide it's better the way it is" (*ID*, 41).

Frank wishes to help Paul and the Markhams by encouraging them to let go of the past and learn, or relearn, independence—what Emerson calls in "Experience" "the capital virtue of self-trust."[1] The methods he chooses to use in pursuing this end are essentially pragmatic ones. He does not argue that the way they see themselves and the world is false and another way is true (i.e., more in accord with the way things really are), because his optimistic belief in mutability means he does not believe that there is any permanent way in which things really are. Instead, he suggests that there may be other ways of seeing the world that are just as accurate (or inaccurate) but that will make them happier than they presently are. Richard Rorty suggests that intellectual and moral progress occurs when one dominant metaphor or vocabulary is replaced by another richer or more interesting one.[2] And this, on a smaller, more personal scale, is precisely the sort of change Frank is attempting to effect. The only thing that will save the Markhams, he tells us, is for them to "figure out a way to think about themselves and most everything else *differently*; formulate fresh understandings based on the faith that for new fires to kindle, old ones have to be dashed; and based less on isolating, bone-headed obstinance and more, for instance, on the wish to make each other happy without neutralising the private self" (*ID*, 90). In order to get the Markhams to think differently in this way, Frank is required to replace, or help *them* replace, their old, unhelpful metaphors with newer, potentially more helpful ones.[3] This process becomes explicit when Joe Markham, while experiencing a psychological crisis in which he understands his failure to buy a house as part of a larger existential malaise ("I've completely quit becoming"), tells Frank that he likes "to have a view of things from above" (*ID*, 50). Frank initially finds this comment mysterious, but he returns to it later in the conversation when he offers an alternative metaphor of his own: "Maybe you ought to try looking at things across a flat plain. . . . I've always thought that looking at things from above, like you said, forced you see all things as the same height and made decisions a lot harder. Some things are just bigger than others. Or smaller" (*ID*, 54). To desire to see things from above, as Joe does, is to seek what Rorty calls a "God's eye view," a complete and total picture in which everything is included. It is to seek, in other words, an impregnable position of knowledge, a complete and universal language, in which contingency, chance, and change can have no effect. For both Rorty and Frank Bascombe, the desire to achieve such a viewpoint (which can never finally be achieved) creates unnecessary problems, problems that can best be solved not by trying, as philosophers traditionally have, to constantly seek a higher and "truer" position but by replacing one (vertical) metaphor with another (horizontal) one. As Rorty argues, "The idea of a 'God's eye view' to which science continually approximates is of a piece with the idea of 'the moral law' to which social custom, in periods of moral progress, continually approximates. . . . Both ideas are to be replaced, pragmatists think, by metaphors of width rather than of height or depth."[4] To give up the "higher" position, to see things "across a flat plain," is to abandon a fantasy of transcendence or totalization and to accept, and be prepared to work within, the inevitable limitations of any particular viewpoint or (to slightly shift the metaphor) language game.[5]

Frank's task with Paul is similar in nature but, because Paul is both a teenager and his son, significantly weightier and more challenging. Frank, from the beginning, doubts his ability to find a new vocabulary that Paul will understand and wish to adopt: "The worst of being a parent is my fate, then: being an adult. Not owning the right language . . . the fate of knowing much yet having to stand like a lamppost with its lamp lit, hoping my child will see the glow and venture closer for the illumination and warmth it mutely offers" (*ID*, 17). Although Frank's conscious intentions with Paul remain pragmatic (he imagines his task as being not to lecture Paul about life but rather to raise "a canopy of useful postulates above him like stars and [hope] he'll connect them up to his own sightings and views like an astronomer" [*ID*, 289]), as their trip to the Baseball Hall of Fame in Cooperstown unfolds, Paul's infuriating resistance pushes Frank in practice away from his principles and toward other, ultimately less useful tactics. In Paul's case it seems possible that the weight of the personal and familial past is simply too heavy to yield to moderate, pragmatic solutions. Frank insists that he and Paul share an interest in "the fissures between the literal and the imagined" (*ID*, 343)—precisely, one would expect, the point where old, outdated ways of thinking can give way to fresh, new ones—but in practice this shared interest, instead of producing newness and change, only sends them back to the futile punning and word games of Paul's "lost childhood": "*Take it for granite. A new leash on life. Put your monkey where your mouse is*" (*ID*, 343, emphasis in the original). Similarly, Frank's attempt to encourage Paul to read Emerson's "Self-Reliance" (the urtext of American pragmatism) ends as Paul mocks Emerson's verbosity and then deliberately rips out one of the pages of his father's treasured copy ("'I just took a page from your book'" [*ID*, 291]). By the time they arrive in Cooperstown, New York, Frank has crucially compromised his ambitions: instead of encouraging Paul to forget the past, Frank has begun trying to replace

Paul's bad, unhappy memories with newer, better ones. When Paul gloomily asks, "What good is it to come to some beautiful place?" (i.e., Cooperstown), Frank responds, "The basic idea, I guess, is you'll remember it later and be a lot happier. . . . So if you've got some useless or bad memories this'd be a great place to start off-loading them" (*ID*, 350).

Cooperstown as the Mecca of American nostalgia—a place dedicated to memories of the most cheerful, sentimental kind—seems to Frank the perfect place for inculcating this new, brighter version of the past. And the fact that such memories, like Cooperstown itself, may lack a certain authenticity does not trouble him; indeed, it strikes him in some ways as a potential advantage:

> Some suspicion lurks . . . that the town is just a replica (of a legitimate place), a period backdrop to the Hall of Fame or to something even less specific, with nothing authentic (crime, despair, litter, the rapture) really going on no matter what civic illusion the city fathers maintain. (In this way, of course, it's no less than what I imagined, and still a potentially perfect setting in which to woo one's son away from his problems and bestow good counsel—if, that is, one's son weren't an asshole.) (*ID*, 293)

This description clearly links Cooperstown to the postmodern, hyperreal American landscapes most famously described in the work of Fredric Jameson and Jean Baudrillard, and Frank's embrace of Cooperstown seems to suggest an alliance between Emersonianism and postmodernism on the basis of a shared rejection of "authenticity" and a shared faith in the virtues of self-creation.[6] Such a linkage, however, as the novel soon makes plain, is clearly a mistake. Philosophically, Frank has taken a wrong turning since the urge to impress good memories over bad ones, however apparently attractive, assumes that memory and the past rather than the future remain the crucial components of individual identity—and for an Emersonian pragmatist to concede this is to, in effect, concede almost everything.[7]

Not surprisingly, then, the new tactics do not work—the past, however spruced up or reconceptualized, cannot be a good guide to the future. Ford signals both the theoretical weakness and the practical collapse of Frank's modified method when, while they are watching a fantasy baseball camp at Doubleday Field, Paul calmly asks Frank whether he was ever abused as a child: the "good" false memories of Cooperstown are, in other words, decisively trumped by other, equally false, but much worse ones. Since neither version of the past is either truer or more convincing than the other, Frank is left in a helpless and hopeless position: "A dead spot now seems to be where these two days have delivered us . . . before I've said enough, before I've achieved a desired effect. . . . Before I've made of this day a memory worth preserving" (*ID*, 352–53).

Frank's failure at this point in the novel (with both Paul and the Markhams) raises the important question of how improvements *can* be effected or understood using a pragmatic method—without, in other words, appealing, as philosophers and moralists traditionally do, to a set of fixed truths or an idea of the way things "really are."[8] Frank's efforts thus far have been based on a faith in the power of words to reimagine and in some sense remake experience. His ex-wife Ann's criticisms of him in this regard are especially illuminating in that they emphasize the Romantic and writerly quality of these tendencies: "Everything's in quotes with you, Frank. Nothing's really solid. Every time I talk to you I feel everything's being written by you. Even my lines" (*ID*, 184). Although Frank is no longer a writer, he remains, albeit in a much diluted and ironized way, a version, or would-be version, of Harold Bloom's "strong poet," the man or woman who is able to remake the world and himself or herself through an act of will or imagination.[9] Another remark by Ann in the same conversation makes the pedigree of these notions even clearer: "You just want everything to seem perfect and everybody to seem pleased. And you're willing to let *seem* equal *be*." The allusion (unconscious presumably on Ann's part) is to Wallace Stevens's famous line in "The Emperor of Ice Cream": "Let be be finale of seem."[10] Ann, as a Michigan literalist committed to a commonsensical notion of reality, has no time for such ideas, but Frank through the bulk of the novel sticks with them, arguing against Ann that the grand abstractions that she considers crucial are much less important and real than the small-scale acts of goodwill and creativity in which he places his own faith: "You're one of those people who thinks God's *only* in the details, but then if they aren't the precise right details, life's all fucked up. You invent things that don't exist, then you worry about being denied whatever they are. And then you miss the things that *do* exist" (*ID*, 254).

Although Frank's ideas are persuasive (and the novel certainly suggests that they are preferable to Ann's), the imaginative edifice that he seeks to create, the truth he attempts to make, is clearly at best—as the title of Stevens's poem emphasizes—a fragile and paradoxical thing.[11] His efforts with Paul and the Markhams, as I have mentioned, fail, and in the end, the kind of change that Frank has been striving to encourage or provoke through language finally occurs on its own, nonlinguistically, without his contrivance and without warning or explanation. The trip to Cooperstown ends when Paul is seriously injured when he is struck in the eye by a baseball: "The machine . . . squeezes another ball through its dark warp, out through the sprightly air, and hits my son full in the face and knocks him flat down on his back with a terrible, loud *thwock*. After which everything changes" (*ID*, 361).

It is at this crucial moment that the novel touches the limits of the American pragmatist tradition. Frank describes Emerson as "the optimistic fatalist" (*ID*, 264), yet for pragmatism, especially neopragmatism, it has tended to be the optimistic side of the Emersonian inheritance that is emphasized—his belief in continual self-creation and the transcendence of limits—with his fatalism being either downplayed or, when recognized, understood as an unfortunate falling off. In this regard "Experience" and especially the famous description in that essay of Emerson's response to the death of his son Waldo is especially relevant. Traditional readings of "Experience," beginning with Stephen Whicher's hugely influential *Freedom and Fate*, suggest that the apparent reserve of this passage indicates in fact the *strength* of Emerson's reaction to his son's death. According to this interpretation, "Experience" marks the decisive turning point in Emerson's work, a shift from an emphasis on individual freedom and toward an emphasis on the opposite tendency, fate or necessity.

Neopragmatist readings of "Experience," on the other hand, tend to emphasize the continuities between early and late Emerson and to suggest, in consequence, that the coolness of Emerson's reaction to Waldo's death should be taken to a large degree at face value—a sign, in Mark Edmundson's words, of his "abiding project, the acquisition of power."[12] Richard Poirier notes, for example, that "Emerson could not mourn for long the deaths of sons and lovers, of Waldo or of Ellen, because his work from the beginning has already celebrated the fact that the Universe—and he, Emerson, who is on its side—can afford to be indifferent to the human presence even while being enhanced by it."[13] For Poirier, Emerson's allegiance is finally more to "Power" and "Action"—to the famous "shooting of the gulf"—than to any particular person. As a position this is certainly logical (family bonds are, after all, deeply conventional), but it may also be ethically troubling. Edmundson, working the same neopragmatist vein, concedes that his conclusions are "disturbing" but makes an essentially similar point: "Although his [Emerson's] loss is too grievous to convert to gain in the space of a single utterance, with a rhetorical flourish, the objective remains an expeditious freeing of the energies of the self, their orderly withdrawal from a bankrupt object. . . . This labor of grief, for Freud and for Emerson who in "Threnody" calls up a sequence of images of his boy in order, symbolically, to slay each one, is most brutally and compellingly described by Nietzsche. It is the labor of transforming 'thus it was' into 'thus I willed it.'"[14]

Such sophisticated coolness in the face of a profound loss gives some fuel to the long-standing criticism that American pragmatism lacks a proper sense of the tragic and that its optimism is, in that sense, naive and partial.[15] It is precisely at moments of peril and suffering, when human beings experience their own limitations, that pragmatism, it seems, may lose some of its purchase. As Richard Rorty admits, the world "can blindly and inarticulately crush us; mute despair, intense mental pain, can cause us to blot ourselves out. But that sort of power is not the sort we can appropriate by adopting then transforming its language, thereby becoming identical with the threatening power and subsuming it under our own more powerful selves."[16] For Rorty, however, these limitations are not cause for embarrassment or concern. Instead, they are a reminder that philosophy is always a human activity rather than an uncovering of the deeper structure of reality. Although those forms of nonhuman power exist, it is pointless, he suggests, to emphasize or dwell on them, because they cannot be helpfully or interestingly rewritten. As I suggested in the introduction, Rorty's views represent only one, strongly antirealist wing of the pragmatist tradition. In the work of James and Dewey, the world beyond or outside language is accorded a significantly larger role. Yet, even allowing for these important internal differences, pragmatism as a whole retains an optimistic outlook in which confusion is usually understood as a prelude to fresh forms of understanding. In *Independence Day*, however, the experience of suffering cannot be quite so easily diminished or put aside. Humans, as Rorty correctly points out, may not be able to rewrite nonhuman circumstances, but the Cooperstown incident suggests the alarming (although perhaps not too surprising) possibility that circumstances may rewrite *us.* "There is no *seeming* now," Frank notes as Paul is being taken to hospital. "All is *is*" (*ID*, 369). And then a little later, when they arrive: "Here is the voice of the *outer* world become primary. . . . While mine—the silenced voice of worry, love, patience, impatience, comradeship, thoughtlessness, understanding and genial acquiescence—is the small voice of the old small life losing ground" (*ID*, 382).

Paul's baseball injury, like Ralph's death, which it painfully echoes, reminds us that the Emerson who presides over *Independence Day* is the author not only of "Self-Reliance" but also of the much more gloomy "Fate," an essay in which the limitation, even irrelevance, of human endeavor in the face of arbitrary nonhuman forces is made extremely plain: "We cannot trifle with this reality, this cropping-out in our planted gardens of the core of the world. No picture of life can have any veracity that does not admit the odious facts. A man's power is hooped in by a necessity, which, by many experiments, he touches on every side, until he learns its arc."[17] The existence of such "odious facts," although downplayed or dismissed by many neopragmatists, remains an abiding concern of the Bascombe novels. The trilogy begins on the anniversary of Ralph's death, and in the opening pages of *The Sportswriter* Frank observes ominously that "for your life to be worth anything you must sooner or later face the possibility of terrible, searing regret. Though you must also manage to avoid it or your life will be ruined" (*S*, 4). While American pragmatism, broadly speaking, emerges and explains itself as a response (whether romantic, scientific, or ironic) to the accumulated failures of a received philosophical and cultural tradition, Frank's pragmatism emerges primarily as a response to personal calamity. It is a crucial difference. The conflict between optimism and gloom, freedom and fate—between a forward-looking, New World meliorism and a much darker, more tragic, and backward-looking vision that we might associate with Europe and the past—is a familiar element of an American narrative tradition that owes as much or more to Hawthorne and Melville as it does to Emerson, but the Bascombe trilogy replays this long-running conflict in a new and distinctive way. Frank's pragmatism, despite its indefatigable and occasionally desperate energy, never completely escapes its own traumatic origins. The action of all three of the Bascombe novels thus involves Frank in a repeated movement away from, then back toward, the experience of grief or mourning. It involves him, in other words, in a continual pragmatic effort to forget that continually fails and yet is always returned to again (albeit in modified form) as the best or only available option.[18]

The final section of *Independence Day*—itself titled "Independence Day," as if after the events of Cooperstown everything, including the novel itself, is forced to somehow begin again—involves a symbolically complex effort to rethink Frank's pragmatic project (and to rethink the key term "independence") so as to make it once again useable. A primary element of this is the reconsideration of the relationship between the private and the public, the individual and the communal. As Frank notes regarding the July Fourth holiday:

> It is an odd holiday to be sure—one a man or woman could easily grow abstracted about, its practical importance to the task of holding back wild and dark misrule never entirely clear or provable; as though independence were *only* private and too crucial to celebrate with others; as though we should just get on with *being* independent, given that it is after all the normal commonsensical human condition, to be taken for granted unless opposed or thwarted, in which case unreserved, even absurd measures should be taken to restore or reimagine it (as I've tried to do with my son, but that he has accomplished alone). Best maybe just to pass the day as the original signers did and as I prefer to do, in a country-like setting near to home, alone with your thoughts, your fears, your hopes, your "moments of reason" for what new world lies fearsomely ahead. (*ID*, 425)

Frank's emphasis here on the private nature of independence may well signal a desire to escape from the recent intrusions of the outer world—to rediscover a space where the pragmatic project as previously imagined may be safely returned to. However, this desire (with its nostalgic and pastoral overtones) is explicitly undercut by the dramatic context in which it occurs. Frank, as he ponders, is watching and taking an interest in the preparations for the Haddam Independence Day parade, a very *public* expression of self-reliance. He is clearly at this point in two minds, caught in a classic, perhaps *the* classic, American dilemma of how to detach oneself from convention (to become free) without in the process becoming merely alienated or self-absorbed—the paradox of how, in the broadest terms, to create an independent *nation*.[19] To jettison the past and be truly free of all conventions means moving away from, even abandoning, shared ideas and a shared language, and the project of pragmatic forgetting in that sense is deeply, and perhaps disturbingly, individualistic. At its most extreme, in other words, the Emersonian urge toward independence may imply the fantasy of sheer self-creation in which no form of familial or social influence is recognized or allowed for. Frank glimpses something like this when his stepbrother Irv shows him an old family photograph and Frank fails to recognize either himself or his mother—an involuntary failure of memory that provokes something like a panic attack: "For an instant I lose my breath entirely and almost gasp, which makes me panic that I'm choking and need a quick Heimlich" (*ID*, 392).

This is a deep-rooted dilemma that pragmatist thinkers have reacted to in a variety of ways, ranging from the individualistic emphases of Emerson and James to the more communitarian ideas of Charles Sanders Peirce and Dewey.[20] In his influential essay "Private Irony and Liberal Hope," Richard Rorty offers a compromise based on the acceptance of an ineradicable public-private division. Although Ford's solution in *Independence Day* is not exactly the same as this, Rorty's ideas offer a helpful way of describing and illuminating the philosophical dimensions of the compromise Frank Bascombe finally does (provisionally) achieve. Rorty accepts that pragmatist ideas are generally most useful in the private realm of self-creation "but pretty much useless when it comes to politics."[21] He suggests that in the public realm the thoroughgoing private skepticism of the pragmatist must be tempered by an awareness of the needs of others, most specifically, their need not to be hurt or humiliated. This balancing act is potentially tricky, he argues, because thoroughgoing skepticism (what he calls "ironism" in this essay) has a great potential to hurt others. Although pragmatism "results from an awareness of the power of redescription," most people, Rorty notes, "do not want to be redescribed." And careless redescription is thus "potentially very cruel."[22] His point is, therefore, that while private acts of redescription can be entirely free, public acts must take careful account of "all the various ways in which other human beings whom I might act upon can be humiliated."[23]

Ford has described *Independence Day* as a novel explicitly concerned with isolation and the difficulty of combining private independence with a larger kind of emotional engagement.[24] And for Frank this dilemma (which is effectively Rorty's public-private dilemma writ small) takes its most forceful form in the question of his relationship with his girlfriend, Sally. In a conversation prior to the Cooperstown incident, Frank answers Sally's question about what it means "to tell somebody you love them" in the following way: "It's provisional. I guess I'd mean I see enough in someone I liked that I'd want to make a whole person out of that part, and want to keep that person around" (*ID*, 168). While this answer is clearly true to Frank's principles—his belief that everything is mutable and nothing permanent—it equally clearly demonstrates little awareness of what Rorty would call Sally's own "final vocabulary" or what we might call, rather more simply, her feelings. On the evening in question it provokes what appears to be the breakup of their relationship, and later on she revisits the remarks, telling Frank that "making her up (which she referred to then as 'reassembling') just to make love appealing was actually intolerable . . . and that I couldn't just keep switching words around indefinitely to suit myself but needed instead to accept the unmanageable in others" (*ID*, 435). Sally, in other words, insists (and Frank accepts) that he must move away from the severity of private irony and toward what Rorty calls "liberal hope," that is, a form of speech and action that, while recognizing there are no permanent truths or human rights, nonetheless seeks to minimize cruelty and harm. "Switching words around indefinitely to suit [one]self" is a reasonable (if dismissive) description of the pragmatic method of making truth rather than finding it, and "accepting the unmanageable in others" is another way of phrasing Rorty's suggestion that "the liberal ironist needs as much imaginative acquaintance with alternative final vocabularies as possible, not just for her own edification, but in order to understand the actual and possible humiliation of the people who use these alternative final vocabularies."[25]

While Rorty argues for a continuing dialectic between private and public —irony and hope—with neither having final priority, Ford's novel (and the Bascombe trilogy in general) suggests a progressive movement, as Frank gets older, away from one and toward the other.[26] This movement is certainly not steady or unequivocal across the three novels, and it involves a good deal of wobbling and falling back on Frank's part, but at the same time it is a clear and recognizable trend. *The Sportswriter* conceives of freedom predominantly as a form of individual escape connected to the possibilities of language and physical movement.[27] *The Lay of the Land*, as I will discuss in chapter 5, suggests a more conservative concern with preserving and fixing meanings in the face of what is beginning to be conceived (individually and culturally) as the threat of impermanence. *Independence Day* as the middle novel of the trilogy offers the Cooperstown incident as the fulcrum or triggering incident of this longer-term shift of emphasis. The awareness of the external world that is first forced on Frank by Paul's injury softens and mutates but never entirely leaves him, and it encourages him, once the first shock has passed, to subtly but significantly modify his previous sense of independence. In the final section of the novel, the project of forgetting is combined, suggestively if paradoxically, with a form of commemoration. Frank goes to visit the site of *Homo haddamus pithecarius*—an old skeleton of unknown origin that has been unearthed during recent construction work—and he is also tellingly reminded by his old friend Carter Knott that July Fourth is the anniversary of the deaths of Thomas Jefferson and John Adams. We might say that in this concluding section the private urge toward self-creation is modified or restrained by an awareness of death as a universal and therefore, in an important sense, shared and public experience. An awareness of individual power, in Emersonian terms, is matched and balanced by an equal awareness of form or fate.

This change of emphasis is most broadly characterized in *Independence Day* as a shift from the "Existence Period" into a new phase, which Frank calls the "Permanent Period." The Permanent Period, which is much more fully explored in *The Lay of the Land*, emphasizes the present rather than the future or the past and is a logical consequence of Frank's discovery that the project of forgetting is circular and self-defeating; that is, that the attempt to jettison loss only leads back to it. (It is also a logical consequence of Frank's getting older and realizing that nonexistence is where we *go to*, as well as where we come from.) "It is another facet in the shining gem of the Permanent Period of life that we try to *be* what we *are* in the present—good or not so good—this, so that accepting final credit for ourselves won't be such a shock later on" (*LL*, 31). As I will discuss in chapter 5, the later novel explores and makes clear the limitations and paradoxes of even the "Permanent Period," but at the end of *Independence Day* it is offered as a new solution, a new way of facing death. Frank tells us that it is

> also possible that I will soon be married, following years supposing I never could again, and so will no longer view myself as the suspicious bachelor, as I admit I sometimes still do. The Permanent Period, this would be, that

> long stretching-out time when my dreams would have mystery like any ordinary person's; when whatever I do or say, who I marry, how my kids turn out, becomes what the world—if it makes note at all—knows of me, how I'm seen, understood, even how I think of myself before whatever there is that's wild and unassuagable rises and cheerlessly hauls me off to oblivion. (*ID*, 450)

On the basis of a passage like this, one may be tempted to wonder whether Frank has abandoned pragmatism completely in favor of a less bold, more complacently bourgeois compromise, but this would be to ignore Ford's clear and persistent efforts to keep his protagonist connected to an Emersonian tradition while at the same time mitigating the more isolating and self-defeating elements of that strategy. The shock of Cooperstown and the bigger, less redeemable losses that these events recalled have not been forgotten about—indeed, the novel has made quite clear that they *cannot* be forgotten about—but neither, the novel stresses, can they easily form the basis of a happily lived life. The novel's carefully considered relationship to loss is formulated one last time in its final pages, when Frank drives past the town cemetery and ponders his own eventual resting place: "On down Pleasant Valley Road along the west boundary fence of the cemetery, wherein tiny American flags bristle from many graves and my first son, Ralph Bascombe, lies near three of the 'original signers,' but where I will not rest, since early this very morning in a mood of transition and progress and to take command of final things, I decided (in bed with an atlas) on a burial plot as far from here as is not totally ridiculous. Cut Off, Louisiana, is my first choice; Esperance, New York, was too close" (*ID*, 439).

Here, space, as so often in American writing, is offered as a solution to the problems of time, but it is a solution that is, in this case at least, surely more subtle (and witty) than it is naive. To remember and recognize loss, Ford seems to be suggesting here, in contradiction to the darker implications of a European philosophical tradition (one may think especially of Heidegger's "being toward death" and other forms of existentialist "authenticity"), does not mean one has to dwell with it or even particularly close to it. To think like that is to give in to morbidity and stasis, to deny the vividness and particularity of life itself. To know that he would one day be buried "at home" near Ralph, Frank says, would "paralyze me good and proper" and would prevent him from fully living out his remaining years. It would indeed be even worse, he goes so far as to suggest in a final clinching metaphor, than "having tenure at Princeton."

To suggest, as I have, that Richard Ford tests the limits of a pragmatic tradition does not mean that he wishes, at least in the Bascombe trilogy, to push beyond those limits into another kind of thinking altogether. There is no sense in these novels (despite their occasional references to the existentialist tradition) of angst leading to insight.[28] This attachment to the here and now may seem simple enough, even simple-minded, yet one of the effects of reading the Bascombe trilogy is to remind us how hard it is to maintain this perspective, this balance, "the high-wire act of normalcy" (*ID*, 94), as Frank calls it, poised between the equally unappealing options of idealism and despair, metaphysics and nihilism. In terms of literary history, the name for this continuing effort is probably realism, but in broader human terms Ford suggests it might be called, after Emerson, self-reliance, or independence, and in that sense the Bascombe novels themselves, in their surprising and subtle variations on their literary and philosophical heritage, are to be read as exemplifications and explorations of this continually American theme.

THREE

"Spoiled People"

Narcissism and the Decentered Self in *Women with Men*

Realist fiction since *Don Quixote* has tended to think of and present itself in opposition to other less truthful modes of seeing and representing the world. Realism as a genre or tendency is, in other words, frequently in a contentious dialogue with other previous or more popular genres against which it wishes to assert its priority. Although the nature of realism's Other changes over time (we might think in the American context of representations of popular theater in Theodore Dreiser, Stephen Crane, and Frank Norris or of Hollywood film in Richard Wright), the pejorative gesture itself is so frequent and so essential to the ongoing and possibly never-ending realist project that it may be seen, as it has been by Fredric Jameson, as one of realism's most prominent and defining characteristics.[1]

In *The Sportswriter*, as I have shown, this realist gesture is largely internalized, as Frank's apparent distrust of literature in general stands in for Ford's more particular desire to distance himself from the tendencies of contemporary neorealism and the presuppositions of his own earlier work. In his more recent short fiction, however, Ford's attention turns more clearly outward, and we get a much clearer, less ironic sense of what he is writing *against*, a clearer awareness, in other words, of the particular kind of falsity or misapprehension that contemporary American culture encourages and that it is the traditional task of realism to rebuff or counter. These various delusory tendencies are never given a single name by Ford, but there is enough evidence in the stories to suggest that they might plausibly be associated with postmodernism as a late twentieth-century intellectual, cultural, and (more complicatedly) psychological phenomenon.

The greatest danger of the postmodern context for Ford is that it encourages and exacerbates the solipsistic tendencies inherent within the broader tradition of American individualism. In the Bascombe novels, these solipsistic tendencies are recognized but also, crucially, balanced and restrained by an awareness of the moral claims of other people. In *Women with Men* and *A Multitude of Sins*, however, such moral restraints have largely disappeared. In these collections of short stories, the private (in the Rortyan sense) overtakes the public, and, as a consequence, the pragmatic acts of self-creation that Ford, via Bascombe, identifies in the earlier novels as necessary to a hopeful or happy life become merely arbitrary and self-serving expressions of personal desire or fancy. When James Wales, one of the protagonists of *A Multitude of Sins*, suggests in response to his lover's complaints about her difficult childhood that "you imagined the past, you didn't remember it. You could just imagine it differently," he is echoing the Emersonian theme of constructive forgetting but also blithely bypassing the inevitable difficulties of such an approach.[2] For Wales, the past is not a burden to cast off or come to terms with but rather an empty space to be filled with more or less anything he chooses.

These stories are less interested in asking whether the self is natural or constructed (since, as I have shown, Ford clearly believes the latter) than they are in exploring the terms and conditions under which self-construction can and should operate. At its most extreme, the postmodern waning of historicity imagines the past and memory as merely a function of a banal but untrammeled will. This new kind of self (as exemplified by James Wales) is appealingly limitless, but in the end, Ford warns, it may not actually be a self at all. As they pursue their self-absorbed pleasures, the protagonists of these two collections are frequently haunted by images of death, dismemberment, and dissolution, images that, as I will argue in more detail in chapter 6, are offered less as moral warnings of what might happen to them if they don't mend their ways than as images of what, in an important sense, they have already become.

In a significant moment in "Occidentals," the third and final story of Ford's 1997 collection, *Women with Men*, Helen Carmichael asks Charley Matthews, her boyfriend and the story's protagonist, what he longs for, and Matthews answers: "I'd like for things not to center so much on me."[3] Afterward this phrase is returned to more than once as a way of explaining what Matthews may or may not want. Not to be at the "center of things," we learn, means, in part, seeking a "less governed life" (*WM*, 157), a life not bounded by social or cultural conventions: "He longed to be less the center of things. He realized this was what a foreign country—any foreign country—could offer you and what you could never get at home. The idea of home, in fact, was the antithesis of that feeling. At home *everything* was about you and what you owned and what you liked and what everybody thought of you. He'd had enough of that" (*WM*, 174–75).

The desire to escape from domesticity and all it represents is a standard-enough trope of male American writing. Leslie Fiedler pointed out more than half a century ago that an urge to "light out for the territory" in one form or another is central to many of the most significant works of the American canon, while, more recently, Philip Fisher and Ross Posnock have both argued in different ways that America and its literature aspire to a condition of permanent immaturity.[4] Charley Matthews has already gone some way to responding to this apparently typical American urge by leaving his job and his marriage and taking a trip to Europe with Helen; as the story progresses, however, it becomes clear that his notions of escape do not follow what we might consider, after Fiedler and others, to be the orthodox patterns.[5] Although Matthews occasionally uses a language of Jamesian self-expansion (he wishes at one point to convert himself "into someone available to take on more of life" [*WM*, 223]), his strongest desire is actually to dissolve or escape from the self rather than to create or embrace a newer or larger identity. Matthews finds Paris, where they are vacationing, baffling and ungraspable, but as the story proceeds he becomes increasingly attracted to it precisely *because* it is a place he will never fully understand and where he could, therefore, never fit in. To live in Paris as he imagines it would be to self-consciously occupy a liminal or marginal position—to be forever undefined and indefinable: "This had to do, he understood, with wanting not to be the center of things, with wanting to get lost in events, with conceivably even fitting into the normalcy of another country—though normalcy, of course, was foolish to think about. Look around (he said this unexpectedly out loud). He could never *fit in* in Paris. Except that was no reason why you couldn't, with the right set of motivations, *be* here" (*WM*, 228).

In this imaginary—selfless and decentered—state, cognitive and communicative disconnection is the necessary precondition for a deeper, more satisfying kind of experience. Matthews comes to regard his limited knowledge of the French language and his lack of curiosity about French culture and history as a means of freeing himself from any kind of social role or responsibility.

> Yet he found there was another, good side to it: since when he would listen in on some conversation Helen was having with a clerk or a flower vendor and would try to figure out from this word or that what either of them were saying, he got almost everything wrong. . . . It could get to be addictive he believed, not understanding what people were saying. Time spent in another country would probably always be spent misunderstanding a great deal, which might in the end turn out to be a blessing and the only way you could ever feel normal. (*WM*, 179–80)

Matthews here associates feeling "normal" with being alienated, and being alienated, in turn, with being free. The basic elements of this linkage may be familiar enough from the various forms of European modernism in which angst is imagined as the unavoidable price of humanness, but Matthews crucially differentiates himself from those traditions by imagining this alienation/normality not as a burden to be endured but rather as a "blessing" to be hoped for. Matthews's desire not to be the center of things is, in other words, much more postmodern than it is modern.[6] It connects, therefore, not only to an established line of American literary individualism but also to a more recent postmodern championing of the decentered subject in contrast to the "centered" or Cartesian self.[7]

If we recognize the literary individualism described by Fiedler, Fisher, and Posnock as being one aspect of a broader Emersonian tendency in American letters, then it becomes perhaps easier to understand the particular combination of ideas that emerge in Matthews's Parisian musings and the particular set of confusions or uncertainties they cause.[8] Emerson's work inaugurated an American pragmatist tradition, a tradition that in turn connected to European postmodernism genealogically (via Nietzsche's reading of Emerson) and intellectually via a shared antifoundationalism. Both ways of thinking reject the notion of a fixed, preexisting truth and argue instead for some version of constructivism.[9] However, while American pragmatism replaces metaphysics with an interest in everyday, contingent, truth-making processes—what Hilary Putnam has called "our sense of the common"—European postmodernism (e.g., in the work of Foucault and Derrida) frequently pushes onward toward something closer to a full-blown relativism in which knowledge becomes merely a function of power, and truth becomes, therefore, something to be avoided or undermined rather than pursued.[10] My contention in this chapter and the next is that in *Women with Men* Ford is alert to the ways in which such relativistic, postmodern tendencies have emerged out of a more homegrown tradition of philosophical skepticism and is concerned with mapping the psychological effects of these tendencies and with suggesting (in terms that ultimately refer back to the American pragmatist tradition) their fundamental weaknesses.

The link between Charley Matthews's views and the perspectives of contemporary postmodernism is suggested most strongly by his relationship with Paris. If Matthews is, or aspires to be, a decentered subject, then Paris, as he sees it, is a decentered and decentering city. From Matthews's perspective there is "nothing natural" (*WM*, 179) about Paris, mainly because, for him, everything about it is mediated through prior representations. Although this is his first visit to France, he previously used the city as a setting in his novel *The Predicament* and discussed it in his classes on African American literature at Wilmot College. The result of all this prior textualization is to make Paris deeply unreal for Matthews ("'I don't really know where any of those places are,' Matthews said. 'I just read about them. They aren't real to me. They never were'" [*WM*, 166]), an effect that he sometimes finds irritating but just as often welcomes as a form of liberation. In the following passage, there are elements not only of Emersonian mysticism (the famous transparent eyeball) but also of a testier, more Nietzschean irrationalism: "In the meantime he felt better about everything. And walking up the wide, congested Boulevard Raspail—a legendary street he knew almost nothing specific about, bound for some unknown destination, with little language available, no idea about currency, distances or cardinal points—made him feel a small but enlivened part of a wider, not a narrower, experience" (*WM*, 222).[11]

Matthews's difficulty in finding his way around the city, which he unsuccessfully attempts to navigate with the help of a Fodor's guidebook, is one of the story's running jokes. His confusion testifies in part to his New World provincialism but also in part, the story suggests, to something inherently puzzling about the city itself. During his final long walk, Matthews wonders whether Paris has a center at all or whether "*downtown* was an American idea, something the French would all laugh at if they knew what he was thinking" (*WM*, 237). The contrast here is not simply between the planned space of the American city and the more organic unplanned space of a European city (since Paris, after Baron Haussmann, is certainly not unplanned) but rather between different forms or degrees of planning.

Philip Fisher, in an unashamedly free-market revision of Henri Lefebvre's critique of capitalist abstraction, argues that the purpose of the American grid system inaugurated by Thomas Jefferson is to eliminate geographical distinctiveness in favor of democratic homogeneity.[12] The grid facilitates movement (both social and physical) by making everywhere more or less the same. Every point on the grid is equal; therefore, every point is, in some sense, the center. The center, in other words, is *everywhere*. According to Fisher, this means it is, symbolically at least, almost impossible to get lost: "This is the special intelligibility and transparency of ways of life that conquered the geographical variety of the American continent, making the American suburb broadly similar from Boston to Los Angeles. It feels 'like' home everywhere."[13] Fisher's version of a homogeneous and democratic America is, to a large extent, a procapitalist fantasy, but it is a telling one. If the American grid system aspires to make everyone feel at home, to make them feel, in other words, perpetually centered, then Paris for Matthews does and means exactly the opposite: it is the place where he can *never* feel at home but where, as a result, he might, possibly, feel most free.[14] Fisher intriguingly describes the new democratic social space created by the American grid as "Cartesian,"[15] and this linkage between geography and philosophy is reinforced toward the end of Matthews's walk when he observes that "ahead of him . . . was St.-Germain-des-Prés and, he'd deduced, the Deux Magots, the Brasserie Lipp, the Café de Flore—one of the great confluences of Europe. There was no more famous place. *Descartes was buried in the church.* It would have to be the center of something" (*WM*, 237, my emphasis). If St.-Germain has to be "the center of something," we might deduce, from its particular philosophical associations, that it is, for Matthews at least, the center of a kind of centerlessness—and this moment is indeed the apogee of his efforts at urban self-erasure. It is followed by an awkward phone call to an ex-lover and then by his discovery that Helen has committed suicide in his absence—the moment of climactic reversal in which the moral failure of Matthews's strategy is definitively exposed.

It is the failure of his relationship with Helen that most clearly expresses within "Occidentals" the philosophical inconsistencies of Matthews's postmodernist position. Matthews's fantasy of escaping from the self is unfavorably contrasted with Helen's desire to hold on to life in the face of a serious, possibly terminal illness. Quite soon after Charley's statement about not wanting to be at the center of things, the two of them have the following exchange:

> "Do you love Paris now?" she said. "Do you feel like you're not the center of everything? Because you're certainly not."
>
> "I don't feel much like it's Christmas."
>
> "That's because you're not religious. Plus you're spoiled," Helen said. "For spoiled people the real thing's never enough. Don't you know that?"
>
> "I don't think I'm spoiled," Matthews said.
>
> "And spoiled people never do. But you are though. . . . Not to want to be at the center of things, that's what spoiled people *think* they want." (*WM*, 180–81)

This conversation takes place in a religious curio shop where Helen has just discovered and purchased (to Matthews's bemusement) a tea towel with the slogan "THE GLORY OF GOD IS TO KEEP THINGS HIDDEN." If Matthews's viewpoint is broadly postmodern, Helen's, as suggested here and reinforced elsewhere, is commonsensically Kantian—she believes there is something like an ultimate truth, but she is also well aware that she does not have direct access to it. Whereas Matthews sees Paris as pleasingly unknowable, Helen sees it as the repository of a kind of seriousness she envies but cannot hope to emulate:

> "You know what people want when they come to Paris?" Helen said, still staring up at the glowing dome with the white sky in the background.
>
> "I don't," Matthews said. "I have no idea."
>
> "To be French," Helen sniffed. "The French are more serious than we are. They care more. They have a perspective on importance and unimportance. You can't become them. You just have to be happy being yourself." (*WM*, 177–78)

If to be French is to be inherently serious, then to be spoiled, it seems, may be typically American—Helen importantly admits that *she* is spoiled too: "I'm the same way. I'm just not as bad as you are" (*WM*, 181). Although Helen may not be free of this besetting problem, she is certainly alert and self-conscious enough to accurately diagnose and describe it. For Matthews and people like him, she tells us, the "real is not enough"—in other words, his postmodern desire to escape from himself (and from meaning more generally) is based on a lack of appreciation for what he already has and a consequently unrealistic or childish yearning for something else. Helen's diagnosis here is a homespun version of the arguments of more sophisticated antipostmodernists such as Hilary Putnam and Jürgen Habermas. For Putnam and Habermas, contemporary relativisms are inherently contradictory, since if *everything* is relative, then relativism itself must be relative also. Therefore, in arguing *against* the universal claims of reason and Enlightenment and arguing *for* the superior claims of relativism, relativists implicitly (or ungratefully, in Helen's terms) assume the existence of the very rational and transcultural standards of proof that they explicitly try to reject.[16]

The cultural and psychological sources of such postmodern relativism are many and complex, and any attempt to precisely define or fix them is far beyond the scope of this study. Nonetheless, Putnam makes a passing remark about this subject that in the context of Ford's work is both relevant and suggestive. Having noted that contemporary skepticism about interpretation is based on an "adolescent sort of error" that imagines that because descriptions can never be complete they are therefore worthless, he then goes on:

> It must be conceded that the error has deep roots. Talk of "otherness," "exotopy," and "incommensurability" would not be as widespread as it is if the ideas of perfect knowledge, of falling short of perfect knowledge, and of the falsity of everything short of perfect knowledge did not speak to us. What those roots are is a matter for speculation. Certainly there is a desire for what psychoanalysts call "fusional" relationships. It is a commonplace to say that the tragedy of life is that we are "alone," that such relationships are impossible; but perhaps as one grows older one comes to feel that separateness as a blessing as well as a curse.[17]

Putnam's suggestion here interestingly illuminates Helen's assertion that Matthews is "spoiled." If the postmodern rejection of the real originates in a frustrated desire for metaphysical "oneness," then it is plausible to see the postmodern gesture not only as a rebellion *against* metaphysics but also (and I suspect this is Putnam's point) as a displaced version *of* it.[18] Matthews's apparent desire to be nothing in this context becomes only a modified version of the standard narcissist's desire to be everything, since both tendencies are based on an unwillingness to recognize the reality of a separate, limited self existing within a world of external objects—a world that contains other people who are both distinct and real. Matthews's desire to escape from himself is, in other words, as Helen's comments perceptively suggest, based on a refusal to be satisfied with what he has and what he, like everyone else, inevitably is.

According to Melanie Klein (following on from Freud), narcissistic disorders are a result of the infant's unsuccessful separation from the mother due to a failure of the Oedipal process. This developmental failure produces feelings of overpowering rage and fear within the patient, feelings that are dealt with by a form of splitting, whereby the bad part of the mother is externalized and the good part is introjected and thus forms the basis of a delusionary and grandiose self-image.[19] If Matthews's desire to lose himself in and be absorbed by Paris is, as I have suggested, a displaced form of narcissism, then we must trace these narcissistic tendencies back not literally to the months of early infancy (rarely a good subject for realist fiction) but rather more simply to Matthews's feelings of emotional abandonment subsequent to the departure of his wife, Penny, and the failure of Blumberg, his French editor and a symbolic father figure, to offer him any adequate compensation for this loss.[20]

Early in the story Matthews remembers his marriage in terms that strongly recall the symbiotic mother-infant bond: "The two of them had once been so close as to be two parts of one person. That was years ago. Whatever he'd liked then she'd liked. Though that was over now" (*WM*, 169–70). He then immediately compensates for this painful recollection of primal loss by reimagining Paris *itself* as a kind of substitute mother/wife: "Paris . . . seemed to lie forth more the way he would've wanted had he ever let himself want it. A metropolis of bounteous issue; a surface to penetrate; a depth in which to immerse oneself, even reside in" (*WM*, 170). In merging or potentially merging with the city, Matthews escapes in fantasy from the loss of Penny and from the murderous anger that loss has provoked in him—a tactic we see in full in the final movement of the story. Within this complicated psychic drama, Helen becomes (in symbolic opposition to Paris) another version of Penny, that is, the "bad" or failed mother whose own needs and desires oppose and take precedence over those of the child (Matthews):

> Helen dominated life, shoved other interests aside, visualized her own interests clearly and assumed his were the same. . . .
>
> The best thing to say about Helen was that he wasn't adequate to her needs and demands, due to needs and demands of his own, and that he should let things go on as they now would, then quietly part company with her once they were home. He'd felt the very same—that he'd barely escaped with his life—when he left behind being a professor. (*WM*, 222)[21]

In this context, Matthews's oddly casual attitude to Helen's cancer ("Helen had had cancer of the something a year before" [*WM*, 158]) can be understood in part as a result of his unconscious feelings of aggression toward her, feelings that are themselves a projection of his more fundamental anger toward Penny. The fantasies he enjoys while walking alone in Paris, fantasies of never going back to the hotel, of abandoning Helen entirely ("just having a long lunch alone, buying the cigar he'd imagined and setting off on a very, very long walk" [*WM*, 238]), suggest that her eventual suicide, although literally unexpected, may also express Matthews's deeper matricidal desires. (This possibility is reinforced by the fact that Helen's actual death in Paris echoes Penny's fictionalized death in Matthews's novel *The Predicament*, where Greta, who is an "unflattering" version of Penny, is killed off in a traffic accident.)

The possibility, suggested by "Occidentals," that postmodern relativism and regressive anxiety are linked responses to a contemporary male experience of loss or absence is also explored in the collection's first story, "The Womanizer," via the relationship between Martin Austin and Joséphine Belliard.[22] Austin, like Matthews, has separated from his wife and is defined by a general dreaminess and lack of intellectual and emotional fixity. Vacillation and uncertainty are his dominant characteristics throughout the story. He second-guesses himself compulsively: "He almost said 'I love you' into the receiver. But that would be a mistake, and he didn't say it, though part of him furiously wanted to. Then he nearly said it in French, thinking possibly that it might mean less than it meant in English. But again he refrained. 'I want to see you very much,' he said as a last, weak, compromise" (*WM*, 39). In contrast,

Joséphine has, we are told, "a greater sense of responsibility than he had; a greater apprehension of life's importance, its weight and permanence" (*WM*, 91). (In other words, within the logic of the story, and perhaps of the collection as a whole, she is characteristically French.) Austin's attraction to Joséphine lacks the kind of unconscious aggression we see in Matthews's relationship with Helen but is nonetheless peculiar in ways that suggest it is equally regressive and narcissistic.[23] First, his desire for Joséphine is almost entirely oral: they never sleep together, and the most physical intimate moments of the relationship are all to do with kissing. Second, Joséphine is throughout extremely, perhaps definingly, resistant and/or indifferent to his oral advances. As a result of these two linked tendencies, Austin spends a significant time in the story trying to maneuver Joséphine into kissing him and then, once he has in some sense succeeded, considering in detail the (usually disappointing) nature of that experience. One example out of several will suffice:

> "I want to kiss you the right way, not that way," Austin said. He pulled her firmly to him again, taking hold of her soft waist and pushing his mouth toward hers. He kissed her as tenderly as he could with her back stiff and resistant, and her mouth not shaped to receive a kiss but ready to speak when the kiss ended. Austin held the kiss for a long moment, his eyes closed, his breath traveling out his nose, trying to feel his own wish for tenderness igniting an answering tenderness in her. But if there was tenderness, it was of an unexpected type—more like forbearance. (*WM*, 71–72)

Joséphine persistently denies Austin the oral satisfactions he craves. She is in that sense, and much more explicitly than Helen Carmichael, the "bad" or withholding mother, just as Austin is (again much more explicitly than Matthews) the disappointed/angry/terrified infant. Austin's unspoken, infantile fears of abandonment are, in the story's final section, partially projected onto Joséphine's actual son, Léo, who is abducted and assaulted after Austin takes him out to a nearby park. The projection is only partial, because in passages such as the following it is clear that the fear of the absent mother is as much Austin's as it is Léo's: "A darker thought entered his mind: of Joséphine *never* coming back, deciding simply to disappear somewhere en route from the lawyer's. That happened. Babies were abandoned in Chicago all the time and no one knew what happened to their parents. He knew no one she knew. He knew no one to contact. It was a nightmarish thought" (*WM*, 77).

If, according to the Putnam passage quoted earlier, both metaphysical realism and postmodern skepticism can be aligned with forms of developmental failure in that both are motivated by an urge for pre-Oedipal "oneness," then Putnam's proposed "solution" of "internal realism" implies a version of successful maturation that involves separation (from the mother or from truth) but not *complete* separation.[24] Such a position clearly echoes the standard Freudian model in which unsatisfiable infantile desire is sublimated in socially useful ways rather than being acted out or repressed. Ford's adherence to this in some ways quite traditional model as an alternative to the developmental failures he associates with the intellectual weaknesses of postmodernism is made explicit in the middle story of the collection, "Jealous," which is set in Montana in 1975 and which acts as a foil to the other two pieces.[25] In contrast to "The Womanizer" and "Occidentals," "Jealous" offers a traditional, perhaps even nostalgic, version of American selfhood in which the inevitable sexual and philosophical uncertainties of adolescence are successfully resolved under the influence of a benign father figure and via the mechanisms of the classical Oedipal model.

The key to the story lies in its initially mysterious title. Although there are some hints of jealousy in the relationships between Larry's father and Larry's aunt Doris and between Larry's father and his estranged wife, these are not particularly significant. The story is clearly not *about* jealousy in any overt or explicit way, and the title only begins to fully make sense when we consider the narrative via a Freudian model in which the relationship between father and son is defined by sexual rivalry over the mother—in which the son is, in other words, by definition, jealous. The structure of the story, in which Larry, the seventeen-year-old protagonist, leaves his father in Montana and travels in the company of his aunt Doris to Seattle to visit his mother, allows what is unspeakable on a conscious level to emerge in the dream-like interval between leaving one parent and reaching the other. The events that occur in and around the Oil City bar, where Doris and Larry are waiting for the Seattle train, function as a fantastic realization of Larry's Oedipal urges. Barney, his aunt's temporary drinking companion, an ersatz father figure, is gunned down by the police, and shortly afterward Doris (who is very clearly a version of the mother) seeks comfort by having sex with Larry in her Cadillac. Larry, in other words, achieves (albeit in a displaced form) what according to Freud every male child truly wants: he satisfies the incestuous desires that, unsatisfied and unsatisfiable, elsewhere in the collection fuel the narcissisms of Matthews and Austin.

The kind of freedom that Doris offers Larry, although it seems exciting and tough-minded at times, is, the story finally insists, regressive and immature. This is signaled strongly, if strangely, by Doris's revelation in the story's final pages that she is bisexual: "I was involved with another woman for a while. Quite a while in fact. It was very fulfilling. . . . Does that shock you? I'm sure it does" (*WM*, 143). Although Larry pretends he isn't shocked by this, he certainly is, and it is this revelation rather than any more orthodox Freudian threat of symbolic castration that has the effect of resolving or ending Larry's Oedipal phase—of allowing him to achieve a healthy and independent selfhood. In using homophobia as the catalyst for successful individuation, Ford appears to be following Freud's suggestion that homosexuality represents a form of narcissistic self-regard.[26] (An implication that is also present in "The Womanizer," where Austin, while in Paris, uncomfortably occupies the apartment of a gay acquaintance, "a luxurious metal-and-velvet faggot's lair with enormous mirrors on the bedroom ceiling" [*WM*, 53].) Such a linkage, between narcissism and homosexual desire, feels outdated in the light of contemporary queer theory, and it may well add to our sense of "Jealous" as a relatively conservative story in which nostalgic regionalism and father-son bonding are offered as implicit alternatives to the failures of postmodern culture.[27] Within the context of the collection as a whole, however, it is important to note that this more old-fashioned vision offers little concrete hope or help to characters such as Austin and Matthews whose social and familial backgrounds have clearly not prepared them to understand or resist the temptations of a contemporary postmodern milieu. If "Jealous" succeeds in reminding us that the dilemmas of the American present are not necessary or universal, that they emerge from a particular historical set of circumstances, it does little to explain how those dilemmas can currently be overcome. For that we must turn again to the endings of the other two stories and in particular to the remarkable penultimate scene of "Occidentals," in which Matthews finally meets his translator, Madame de Grenelle.

Part of the purpose of the scene between Matthews and Madame de Grenelle is certainly to mock Matthews, perhaps on some level even to morally punish him for his previous blindness and self-absorption. If through most of the story (focalized as it is through him) we have seen other people—Helen and Penny especially—translated into his way of thinking, this pattern is comically reversed by Madame de Grenelle, who proposes to transform Matthews's self-justifying autobiographical novel into a satire with an unreliable protagonist:

> "So. It is not quite finished in English. Because you cannot rely on the speaker. The *I* who was jilted. All the way throughout, one is never certain if he can be taken seriously at all. It is not entirely understandable in that way. Don't you agree? Perhaps you don't. But perhaps he has murdered his wife, or this is all a long dream or a fantasy, a ruse—or there is another explanation. It is meant to be mocking."
>
> "That could be true," Matthews said. "I think it could." (*WM*, 253)

Madame de Grenelle's subversive rereading of *The Predicament* functions also and equally well as an interpretation of "Occidentals" itself, since Matthews's moral reliability is central to both the imagined novel and the actual story. In that sense, this scene could be seen as itself a postmodern gesture by which Ford emphasizes the status of the story as only one text (among other texts) by including within it its own ironic reinterpretation. Madame de Grenelle's otherness in relation to Matthews is strongly signaled by both her race and her sexual orientation, and at first or even second reading it may seem that her intervention at this late stage shows Ford conceding to the relativizing, postmodernist tendencies that the rest of the story seems to wish to resist.[28] Madame de Grenelle is brutally accurate in some ways but crude and coercive in others; in other words, she herself is not entirely reliable, and the temptation may be to conclude from this fact that there is no one right interpretation of what has happened or of who Matthews is and that Ford is offering us finally, in opposition to Matthews's narcissistic fantasies, only a more sternly postmodern and pluralistic world made up of incommensurable language games, of separate versions of the truth that cannot ultimately meet.

At this point, however, it is useful to refer again to Hilary Putnam. In *Reason, Truth and History* Putnam specifically addresses the issue of translation as part of his consideration of relativist arguments concerning incommensurability. He notes that relativists such as Thomas Kuhn and Paul Feyerabend emphasize the impossibility of any true or accurate translation across languages or even across different historical versions of the same language: "The incommensurability thesis is the thesis that terms used in another culture, say, the term 'temperature' as used by a seventeenth-century scientist, cannot be equated in meaning or reference with any terms or expressions *we* possess. As Kuhn puts it, scientists with different paradigms inhabit 'different worlds.'"[29] Putnam rejects these arguments as self-refuting by noting that if they were taken literally, they would mean that people from other eras or cultures (or even earlier versions of ourselves) could not be understood or recognized *at all*. As with other contemporary manifestations of relativism, he sees radical skepticism about translation as being based on the failed fantasy of complete synonymy (which he argues is equally absurd). Rather than the opposed alternative of synonymy or incommensurability, Putnam offers a notion of translation based on "interpretative charity": "Interpretative success does not require that the translatees' beliefs come out the *same* as our own, but it does require that they come out *intelligible* to us."[30]

Although Matthews has, in an earlier conversation with Helen, explicitly supported a relativistic understanding of translation ("I think it's inventing. . . . I think it's using one book to invent another one" [*WM*, 164]), the story's conclusion emphasizes that his opinions have changed. The story ends with Matthews deciding to write a long-delayed letter to his parents: "And in his letter he would try as best he could, and with the many complications that would need detailing, to explain to them all that had happened to him here and what new ideas he had for the future" (*WM*, 255). In writing to his parents, Matthews is clearly "centering" himself again; in other words, he is placing himself firmly back inside the social and historical contexts from which he has earlier sought to escape. This may seem like a modest and rather conservative gesture to the extent that it suggests that the best alternative to relativism is a return to social convention or orthodoxy, but within the logic of the story and in the context of his recent narcissistic and matricidal fantasies it is a small but telling vision of a new maturity (or realism, to use Putnam's term) in which the various experiences of loss, separation, and difference—all symbolically encapsulated in the original loss of the mother—can be acknowledged and managed through (rather than denied or embodied by) language and in which also the very ability and willingness to recognize and communicate with others, however uncomfortable or partial that communication may feel, is itself important evidence of a shared set of assumptions and beliefs.

Such moments of hard-won hopefulness are rare enough in Ford's short fiction, but their rarity testifies more to the difficulties of expressing, even within art, the valuable but unstable combinations of knowledge and uncertainty that internal realism (to use Putnam's term) implies than to any lack of faith or belief on Ford's part in the importance of the realist project. In "Charity," a story in his next collection, *A Multitude of Sins*, the protagonist, Nancy Marshall, while on vacation in Maine finds herself observed by a busload of Asian tourists, who, she is sure, imagine her to be very different from the person she actually is. "Isn't it odd," she says to her husband, "to be seen but to understand you're being seen wrong" (*MS*, 205). This encounter subtly echoes that between Matthews and Madame de Grenelle in the sense that both are moments of cross-cultural encounter in which recognition and misrecognition are combined. Ford's point in the Madame de Grenelle scene is surely that *both* elements of the experience of communication or translation (the being seen *and* the not being recognized) are equally crucial, since to achieve maturity is to recognize both similarity *and* difference, that is, to realize that other people exist but that it is not possible to completely understand them.[31] If to be fully understood (or centered) is the nightmare from which male American protagonists from Rip Van Winkle onward have fled, then Ford reminds us in *Women with Men* and elsewhere that to *not* be understood or seen *at all* (to be decentered) is in fact equally unbearable and impossible. If both "Occidentals" and "The Womanizer" only hint at a third "mature" position, it is not, as I have just suggested, because Ford does not recognize that such a position is real and meaningful but rather because such a position is so inherently unstable and fleeting that to name it at all is to risk having it harden into truth or dissolve into difference. As Nancy notes in "Charity," after being seen but also not seen by the busload of tourists, "It was a grand feeling. . . . The great mistake would be to try to seize . . . and keep it forever. It was good just to know it was available at all" (*MS*, 205).

FOUR

"What Was That Thing She Was?"

Realism, Postmodernism, and the Fragmented Body in *A Multitude of Sins*

In *Women with Men* Ford's exploration of the dangers of a postmodern environment focuses mainly on questions of male self-understanding and self-definition. Whereas in the Bascombe trilogy, Frank Bascombe responds to personal loss by (eventually at least) turning outward and acknowledging and embracing the reality of other people and the external social world, Matthews and Austin both turn inward. They respond to the discomfort of separation or absence by regressing to an infantile fantasy of plenitude and boundlessness. Their narcissism is imagined as in some ways typically American (in contrast to the seriousness and implicit maturity of Europe), but it is also, I have argued, distinctly postmodern in that, especially in Matthews's case, the narcissistic self attains or maintains its grandiosity by, paradoxically, seeking to disappear completely.

Ford's next collection, *A Multitude of Sins*, maintains a critical concern with the postmodern context but shifts and broadens the focus of *Women with Men*. In *A Multitude of Sins* Ford's interests become increasingly ontological. The stories come back again and again to the large and vexing questions of what is and isn't "real." Such questions clearly take Ford back to the eighteenth- and nineteenth-century roots of literary realism, in which the conflict between appearance and reality was central, and the familiar tropes of classic realism are indeed frequently in evidence in the collection, most obviously in its obsessive interest in adultery. I want to argue, however, that Ford is doing more than simply applying old realist methods and ideas to a new historical context (although on occasion that's what he may seem to be doing). In *A Multitude of*

Sins, as in *Women with Men*, Ford recognizes the postmodern problematization of the real as a deep-seated and wide-ranging cultural phenomenon that as a realist he needs to take account of, but he also recognizes the extent to which such a phenomenon complicates and perhaps even undermines the traditional realist project. *A Multitude of Sins* is a complex and sometimes paradoxical collection precisely because it is so alive to the difficulties and strangeness of using inherited realist distinctions (between the true and the false, the real and the unreal) within a context in which those distinctions have been thoroughly and repeatedly ironized.

Ford's efforts in *A Multitude of Sins* to map this new philosophical landscape and to consider the ways in which literary realism might engage with it are clearest and most explicit in "Quality Time," the collection's second story. James Wales, the protagonist of "Quality Time," is a successful journalist who has come to specialize in what he calls instances of "failed actuality." The story's central example of the phenomenon of failed actuality is the funeral of Princess Diana, which Wales goes to London to report but ends up watching on television, since, as he sees it, "it was an event for TV anyway—his reactions were the story" (*MS*, 24). From Wales's point of view, the funeral is a postmodern spectacle, a triumph of false or media-generated emotion in which representation leaves reality behind: "The tabloids had their tombstone headlines up. *WE MOURN! WE GRIEVE! THEY WEEP! GOODBYE!*" Wales concludes his article on Diana's funeral with the observation that "*someone has to tell us what's important because we no longer knew*" (*MS*, 25, emphasis in the original). Wales's job as a self-appointed specialist in failed actuality is, therefore, to tell people what to feel. (As he says himself, "It was not exactly journalism" [*WM*, 16].) He is in a position of authority and knowledge in the sense that he is able to understand and describe what is going on in such postmodern moments, yet that does not mean he is able to escape from the pervading atmosphere of unreality that they contribute to. Turning his reactions into the story falsifies, it seems, both the story *and* his responses to it. Ford shows us Wales as a man fluent and deeply interested in the various signifiers of emotion but detached from anything resembling actual feeling. His adulterous relationship with Jena consists of a series of emotional gestures and poses so empty and so clearly learned that they more than once become inadvertently comical:

> Making love was eventful. At first she was almost dalliant, though selective, vaguely theatrical, practiced. And then after time—though all at once, really—engrossed, specific, unstinting, exactly as if it was all unscripted, all new ground, whatever they did. She could find the new with great naturalness, and he was moved by the sensation that something new could occur with someone: that self-awareness could take you on to immersion and then continue for a long while. He resisted nothing, abjured nothing, never lost touch with her in all of it. It was what he wanted. (*MS*, 23)

This kind of critique of false or heightened emotionality, while very clearly attached to its own historical moment, also has its roots in the attacks on sentimentality and sentimental fiction so common in the great works of nineteenth-century realism. Ford is in that sense offering postmodernism as only the latest in a line of illusory cultural tendencies against which realism must set itself. Behind such a critique of false emotion there must logically lie (as there does in Gustave Flaubert, Henry James, and Jane Austen) a notion of what a more real or more authentic emotional experience might be like. And indeed, in explicit contrast to the falsity of Diana's funeral (and also in more implicit contrast to the emotional falsity of the adulterous relationship between Wales and Jena that takes up the bulk of the story), Ford offers the examples of two other deaths and their aftermaths: the death of the wife of Wales's English friend, which occurs on the same weekend as Diana's funeral and is therefore overshadowed by it, and the death of an anonymous woman in Chicago whom Wales witnesses being hit by a van in the story's opening paragraphs.

If the first of these is openly described by Wales as "real-er" (than Diana's death), then the second is surely offered as the real-est of the three—real-est in the sense that it appears to show us death as a pure, unmediated event, unsullied by representation or interpretation. Its position at the beginning of the story gives it an obvious dramatic weight, and it stands out, most importantly, as the one event in the story that provokes a direct physical response from Wales: "He couldn't see the woman. Though no one was kneeling to assist her—which was a sure sign. His heart began rocketing. Cold sweat rose on his neck in the warm car. He was suddenly jittery" (*MS*, 11). Wales immediately controls these physical reactions by first comparing the woman's death to the death of a photo-journalist, "a man named Peter Swayzee he'd known in Spain . . . a silly man who was dead now, shot to pieces covering a skirmish in East Africa," and then by reassuring himself that his own chosen way of life keeps him at a safe distance from such events: "He himself had never done that—covered a war or a skirmish or a border flare-up or a firefight. He had no wish for that. It was reckless. He preferred the parts that weren't war. Culture. And he was now in Chicago" (*MS*, 11). The contrast at work here—on the one hand, culture, Chicago, adultery, and the notion of failed actuality, on the other, death, violence, war, the Third World, with the latter being real and the former fake—recalls in a fairly straightforward, nonironic way the active, masculine ontology of writers such as Hemingway and Camus.[1]

We can see the story, then, at its most straightforward, as being structured around a simple if powerful opposition between the (real) death of the anonymous pedestrian and the (false) death of the "phony princess," with Wales's and Jena's thoughts and behavior throughout indicating the emotional and psychological consequences of living, even self-consciously, in accord with the latter. "Quality Time" in this sense does what realism in general has always sought to do: it differentiates between appearance and reality, and it reveals the falsity of currently common or dominant ways of thinking and seeing. To that extent it may seem to be an accomplished but also quite anachronistic piece of work that responds to the new, postmodern context mainly by harking back to tropes inherited from a venerable realist tradition and from the more stoical or existential strands of American modernism.

There is, however, I want to argue, rather more to it than that. The death of the female pedestrian is offered as the realest event in the story, but the kind of realness this event possesses or suggests is of a peculiar and not especially "realistic" type. What Ford emphasizes most about the woman's death (besides its ontological weight) is its mysteriousness. This is the story's opening paragraph:

> Where he stopped for the red light on busy Sheridan Road, Wales watched a woman fall down in the snow. A sudden loss of footing on the slick, walked-over hummock the plows had left at the crosswalk. Must be old, Wales thought, though it was dark and he couldn't see her face, only her fall—backwards. She wore a long gray man's coat and boots and a knitted cap pulled down. Or else, of course, she was drinking, he supposed, watching her through his salted windshield as he waited. She could be younger, too. Younger and drinking. (*MS*, 9)

Apart from the fact that she has just fallen over, very little about this woman is certain—she may be young or old, sober or drunk. Although Wales watches her carefully, her behavior strikes him as disjointed and inexplicable: "Who knows what's buzzing in that head, Wales thought, watching. A moment ago she was lying in the snow. A moment before that everything had been fine" (*MS*, 10). A few seconds later, after the woman has been hit by a van and killed, Wales sees her changed "in an instant from an old, young, possibly drunk, possibly sober woman in a gray man's coat, into a collection of assorted remnants on a frozen pavement" (*MS*, 11). The second part of this sentence implies that the difference between life and death is the difference between integrity and dispersal: the woman is *now* a collection of assorted remnants, whereas *before* she was something else, something presumably more coherent and thus more recognizably human. The first part of the sentence, however, ironizes this commonsense suggestion by pointing out that the woman was *already*, while still alive, in pieces, already, while still alive, in some sense a collection of contradictory elements or remnants. On one level this is a witty, slightly ghoulish joke on Ford's part, but if we recall the ontological importance of this incident to the structure of the story, we may see it as even more than that.

In *The Body in Pieces* art historian Linda Nochlin analyzes images of decapitation and dismemberment in French art from the revolution through the nineteenth and early twentieth centuries and concludes that the fragmented body is a key metaphor for modernity itself. Recalling Marx's famous description of the revolutionary power of capitalism ("all that is solid melts into air, all that is holy is profaned"), Nochlin argues that the disintegrated body in painting and sculpture becomes a powerful metonym for the larger political, intellectual, and cultural losses of integrity and cohesion that modernity ushers in. Toward the end of the book she broadens her perspective and offers a brief but highly suggestive account of how this thesis might be brought to bear on the art of the postmodern period. Referring to work by American artists Robert Mapplethorpe, Louise Bourgeois, and Cindy Sherman, Nochlin suggests that "the postmodern body, from the vantage point of these artists and many others, is conceived of uniquely as the 'body-in-pieces': the very notion of a unified, unambiguously gendered subject is rendered suspect by their work."[2] Reading Ford's story in the light of Nochlin's argument, we may see that the fragmented body of the dead pedestrian, rather than offering a stern, realist counterargument against the illusions of the postmodern, is actually itself a version of postmodern subjectivity, a possibility subtly suggested by the fact (already noted) that the woman was no more coherent alive than dead. The disintegrated body of the anonymous woman is, in this sense, just a more solid, corporeal echo of the less tangible but not less real subjective uncertainty of Wales and Jena, both of whom are solipsistic, distracted, and unable ever, it seems, to develop a clear or consecutive line of thought. As seen in the following typical passage, their sense of themselves and each other is vague and baseless, a play of empty signification:

> "Do you still keep your flat in Berlin?" She was just talking still, not paying attention, light-headed after being with him. They were on the street in Chicago, in winter, going for supper late. Saying "keep your flat" must feel good. He'd felt that way. It was like saying, "We live in the Sixth." Or, "It's just off the King's Road." Or "We took rooms behind the Prado." Simple, harmless things.
>
> "Yes. It's in the Uhlandstrasse," he said.
>
> "Is that in the East?"
>
> "No, it's in the rich quarter. Near the Zoo and the Paris Bar. Kudamm. Savignyplatz." She didn't know what these words meant, which was fine. She could hear them. (*MS*, 27)

If the death of the anonymous pedestrian doesn't in the end offer itself (as it initially appears to) as an authentic or natural alternative to the cultural flimsiness of postmodern experience, it does, however, suggest that postmodern experience has two distinct aspects, one of which is much more overtly troubling or grotesque than the other. Although Wales and Jena may have a good deal in common with the dead woman (all three seem to consist of a bundle of disconnected meanings), they are clearly in other, but equally important, ways very different from her. In order to better grasp the particularities of these two different aspects of the postmodern subject, it is useful, following Nochlin, to take a brief detour into the work of Cindy Sherman, an exemplary postmodern artist whose photographs demonstrate and explore these same distinctions and connections.

Nochlin's very brief discussion of Sherman in *The Body in Pieces* focuses on the works in her Sex Pictures series of 1992, in which Sherman built female mannequins out of a variety of plastic and rubber prostheses, masks, and sex toys and then photographed the mannequins in quasi-pornographic poses (figure 1). The Sex Pictures series, like the dead pedestrian in Ford, interprets the dissolution of the postmodern subject as a form of simulacral horror, an eruption of the Freudian uncanny in which humanness has all but disappeared, leaving behind only a macabre memory of itself. Sherman's earlier work of the 1970s and 1980s, however, notably the famous Untitled Film Stills series, addresses broadly similar issues of representation and female identity but does so in very different ways. In the Untitled Film Stills series, identity becomes explicitly performative, a pluralistic masquerade in which the self is both revealed and hidden through the borrowed tropes of American popular film. Sherman appears disguised, dressed up in various kinds of clothes and makeup and placed in a range of situations, all of them strange but all also vaguely reminiscent of the mise-en-scène of the Hollywood movies of Douglas Sirk or Alfred Hitchcock (figure 2). As in Sex Pictures, Sherman is offering the self as a kind of simulacrum built from pieces picked up elsewhere, but a simulacrum rooted in a very different genre—melodrama as opposed to horror.

Hal Foster (writing in 1996) identified this duality in Sherman's work as typical of a strain of "bipolar postmodernism" in which the "simulacral intensities and ahistorical pastiches" most typical of the 1980s began to be replaced by a concern in the work of artists such as Sherman and Andres Serrano with the melancholic, depressive, or abject (Julia Kristeva being the crucial theorist of this latter tendency).[3] Foster sees the postmodern interest in abjection and horror as a reaction against the consumerist fantasies of a "performative postmodernism"—as the expression of a desire not to "delight in the sheer image" but rather to "possess the real thing." As I have already noted in relation to Ford, however, such a return to the real is deeply problematic. The physical body may *seem* more substantial, more real, than weightless images of postmodernity, but the kind of bodies we see in the works of Serrano, Sherman, and others are broken apart, inverted, and traumatized. As Foster wryly notes, it is hard to imagine building an ethical or politically progressive alternative to performative postmodernity on such a basis: "If there is a subject of history for the culture of abjection at all, it is not the Worker, the Woman or the Person of Color, but the Corpse. This is a politics of difference pushed beyond indifference, a politics of alterity pushed to nihility."[4]

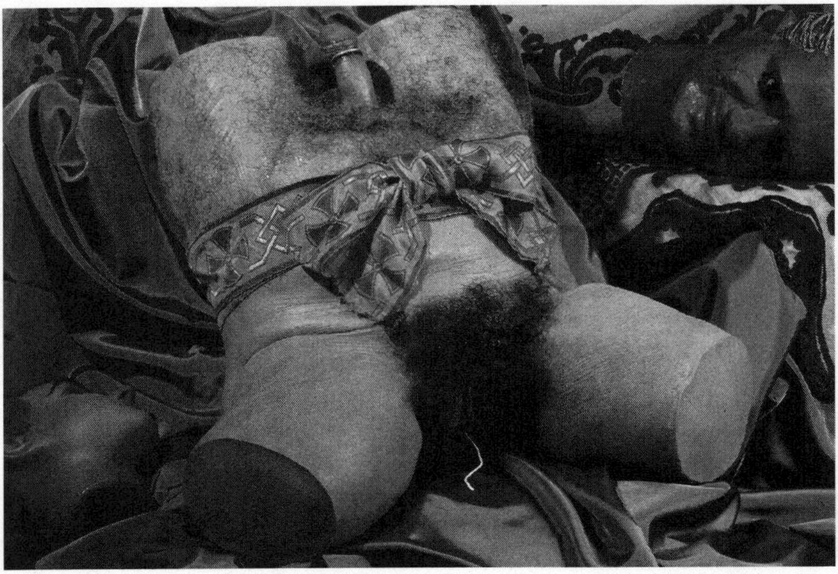

FIGURE 1. Cindy Sherman, #263 (1992), from the Sex Pictures series.

FIGURE 2. Cindy Sherman, #57 (1980), from the Untitled Film Stills series.

This, then, is the odd position Ford as a realist writer finds himself in: he goes looking for an alternative to the postmodern but finds only another (albeit more startling and nihilistic) version of effectively the same thing. It is a dilemma that recurs in a number of places in *A Multitude of Sins*. The collection's final story, "Abyss," for example, concludes with Frances Bilandic, one half of the adulterous couple at its center, suffering a fatal fall into the Grand Canyon as a result of trying to find a perfect place to pose for a photograph: "I want just me and the canyon in the picture. Nothing else. Look through it now. See what you see when you see me" (*MS*, 274). Frances's desire to control her own visual representation here is a mundane echo of the postmodern self-portraiture of Sherman and others. She has turned the canyon into a vast fetish object that despite its obvious emptiness (crudely noted by Howard) becomes for her a vision of the Absolute: "a completely spiritual place," a "great wonder," "full of healing energy."[5] That Howard observes Frances's disappearance through the viewfinder of a camera ("The space he'd had fixed with the viewfinder was there. . . . But Frances was not occupying the space" [*MS*, 274]) emphasizes the extent to which her death marks the failure of a particularly visual fantasy, or, to put it more specifically, the revelation of what that visual fantasy excludes. When Howard puts aside the camera and looks down into the canyon he sees Frances's body, like the body of the pedestrian in "Quality Time," reduced to fragments: "It was her face he saw first, appearing round and shiny in the sunlight. She was staring up at him, her eyes seemingly open, though the rest of her—her white shorts and blue sailcloth top with the anchor, her bare arms and legs—these were all jumbled about her in a crazy way, as if her face had been dropped first, and then the rest of her. It actually seemed, from here, that one arm was intact but separated from her body" (*MS*, 276).[6]

One may well wonder how, or if, literary realism can operate in this new context in which the real is either theatricalized plenitude (the hyperreal) or dismemberment and death. What better, more workable and livable alternatives are, or might be, available? From the perspective of postmodern theory the options appear severely limited. There is no point in looking for a more grounded way of understanding the world, such theory suggests, because no such thing exists. Since what we refer to as "reality" or "truth" is always a man-made, discursive construct, the best that can be achieved are acts of parody or subversion by which less appealing elements of culturally/linguistically constituted reality can, at least for a while, be interestingly or hopefully rejigged.[7] Postmodern culture must, in other words, be met on its own terms, and to wish for or imagine a more solid or grounded way of seeing the world is to betray a desire for old-fashioned metaphysical certainties that are at best delusionary and at worst a disguised means of exercising coercive power.

Ford's response to the postmodern condition is, I wish to argue, subtly but significantly different from this. He does not deny that the self and reality are constructs that cannot exist apart from or outside culture—he does not, in other words, revert to metaphysics—but he understands the socially constructed real in pragmatic rather than postmodern terms. What this means, to put it most simply (and I will say more in a moment), is that he can imagine a version of reality that is grounded in human consensus rather than timeless truth but that is also, crucially, noncoercive and potentially liberating. Evidence for the existence of this pragmatic alternative is certainly not abundant in *A Multitude of Sins*. In "Quality Time" the possibility is hinted at by the "realer" death of the wife of Wales's English friend, yet the story pays almost no attention to this death, and within the collection as a whole this kind of ontological middle ground—where the Bascombe trilogy almost permanently resides—is mainly absent. The important exception to this tendency, however—and, consequently, the key to better understanding the nature of Ford's alternative to postmodernism—is the collection's penultimate story, "Charity," to which I will now turn.

Tom, the husband in "Charity," exemplifies, like most of the other adulterers in *A Multitude of Sins*, a set of distorted and distorting ideas about the self and about what is and isn't real. "Charity" differs notably from the other stories in the collection, however, in that it develops a clear alternative to these ideas via Tom's wife, Nancy. Having moved out of the marital home in Maryland after having a brief affair, Tom has decided that he and Nancy should move together to Maine to make a fresh start. Tom's attraction to Maine (not shared by Nancy) is based on his respect for "authenticity" and his vague but powerfully held feeling that Maine has more of this quality than most other places: "Tom had an affinity for styles of living he considered authentic. . . . He thought highly of the Mainers for renting their seaside houses for two months in the summer and collecting fantastic sums that paid their bills for the year. This was authentic to Tom" (*MS*, 196). Tom's view of Maine as realer than the rest of America ("something hazy about the country having started here and the ocean being 'primary' among experiences" [*MS*, 191]) carries a similar meaning to Frances's admiration for the Grand Canyon in "Abyss." Both Tom and Frances, having sought and failed to locate a better version of reality via adultery, seek it elsewhere by projecting their desires onto a particular place rather than a particular person. What they actually encounter in the canyon and in Maine, however, is the hyperreal. Compared to the knowingness of James Wales, their encounters with hyperreality are deeply unselfconscious—they never realize just how insubstantial it is—yet the stories themselves make the point clearly enough. Although Tom's opinions are not so violently dismantled as Frances's are, they are sharply ironized by the story's opening, which takes place in the early hours of the morning in a B&B opposite the L.L.Bean store in Freeport. The scene establishes Maine (for which L.L.Bean stands as a metonym) as a signifier of a commodified authenticity, a global brand for which naturalness is a key selling point. Tom himself neatly, but entirely unselfconsciously, sums this up when Nancy asks him "why all the people come," and he replies: "I guess they love it. . . . This is what Maine means. A visit to Bean's after midnight. It's the global culture" (*MS*, 180).

"Charity" suggests, then, once again, a direct connection between postmodern experience and adulterous desire.[8] It also, in common with a number of other stories in the collection (including not only "Quality Time" and "Abyss" but also "Puppy" and "Under the Radar"), goes on to associate these twinned tendencies with death.[9] While Tom imagines Maine and adultery as representing life in opposition to death, Nancy sees both the activity and the place as being themselves deathly.[10] When she thinks of Maine she thinks of the story of a woman shot by a deer hunter because she was wearing white gloves while hanging out laundry (*MS*, 192, 211), and when, earlier, Tom confesses to his affair she experiences a disorienting vision of his face transformed into a skull: "His face . . . looked at that moment more like a skull, a death's head" (*MS*, 185–86). However, whereas in "Quality Time" and "Abyss" these connections, once demonstrated, have no significant repercussions (nothing important is learned as a result of the deaths of Frances and the unnamed pedestrian), in "Charity" they prompt the beginning of Nancy's search for an alternative way of thinking and being. When Nancy imagines Tom's face turning into a death's head she also imagines her own sense of identity dissolving: "But what was it, she wondered, as they left the restaurant headed for home and bed? What was that thing she was? Surely it was a thing anybody should be able to say. There would be a word for it. She simply couldn't bring that word to mind" (*MS*, 187).

Nancy's efforts in the remainder of the story to rethink and rebuild a viable, postmarital self are, I want to suggest, essentially pragmatic, and they offer the clearest example of Ford's pursuit of a pragmatic alternative to the unattractive options offered by a bipolar postmodernism. On a simple level, Nancy is unsure of herself in the passage just quoted because she has left one long-standing social role (being Tom's wife) without yet finding another one to step into. Behind that reasonably straightforward suggestion, however, the passage suggests a larger set of presuppositions about the self: first that the self is social or relational—she is uncertain of who she is because her relationships have changed—and second that the self, or self-understanding, is connected to language—finding a new self involves finding the right words.

Postmodern theory of the kind Ford's realism is implicitly critiquing certainly does not deny that the self is linguistically and socially produced—indeed, that is one of its primary claims—but it differs from pragmatism on the issue of how, if that is the case, meanings are made and legitimated within this world of socially and linguistically produced subjects. Whereas postmodernism suggests that meaning is primarily limiting or oppressive, an effect of power or coercion, pragmatism suggests that meaning is (or can be) an effect of conversation and democratic consensus. We might compare, in this regard, Foucault with Dewey and note, as Richard Rorty does in *The Consequences of Pragmatism*, that although the two thinkers have a great deal in common, there are also crucial differences of moral outlook or tone between them. Neither Dewey nor Foucault believes in a fixed human nature. Both emphasize that truth is humanly made. Yet while Dewey argues that the desire to create meaning is generally positive and progressive (for Dewey, Rorty suggests, "the will to truth is not the urge to dominate but the urge to create"), for Foucault that desire is inherently questionable ("[we] must conceive discourse as a violence that we do to things").[11] In some sense this difference is a small one, a matter of emphasis, but the consequences are nevertheless significant.

In "Charity" Nancy begins to build her new self not by attempting to subvert or parody conventional versions of female selfhood, as postmodern theory might suggest is the best or only option, but rather more pragmatically by looking at the world around her and gathering evidence of who she is and isn't—by comparing herself to other people and being alert to the ways other people see and understand, or misunderstand, her. The story's key moment in this regard is the moment already briefly mentioned, when Nancy finds herself seen but misunderstood by a busload of tourists:

> "Do you ever think about what the people in buses think when they look out their window and see you?" she said, watching the bus shudder through its gears up the hill toward a blue Ford agency sign.
>
> "No," Tom said, still peering in at the pictures of houses for sale.
>
> "I just always want to say, 'Hey, whatever you're thinking about me you're wrong. I'm just as out of place as you are.'" She set her hands on her hips, enjoying the sensation of talking with no one listening. She felt isolated again, unapprehended—as if for this tiny second she had achieved yet another moment of getting on with things. It was a grand feeling in that it arose from no apparent stimulus and would no doubt not last long. Though here it was. (*MS*, 205)

This moment, which is approvingly referred to several times later on in the story, offers a miniaturized model of how a pragmatic self can be constructed out of the complex interplay between subject and object. Nancy is not who the tourists think she is, yet at the same time she is "the same as them." She enjoys being isolated and unapprehended, yet the scene makes clear that this isolation is *made* enjoyable by the presence of other people and their attempts to understand her.

Ford is hinting here at the possibility of the self that is relational but also separate and distinct, a self that can only be understood by its connections to other people yet is not completely reducible to those connections. In order to understand the kind of pragmatic balancing act that Ford is attempting to pull off here, it is helpful to compare Nancy's efforts at self-building with the theory of the self proposed by George Herbert Mead, a colleague of John Dewey whose ideas have significantly influenced Jürgen Habermas's critique of postmodern theory.[12] Mead sees the self as a process that always contains the dual elements of "I" and "me." The "me" for Mead is the socially produced self—or, to be more precise, it is the self that consists of an internalization of the attitude of other people, this process of internalization for Mead being the very definition of selfhood: "The taking or feeling of the attitude of the other toward yourself," he argues, "is what constitutes self-consciousness."[13] In tandem with this "me," however, the self also always contains an "I," whose nature is much more mysterious. Mead explains the "I" as being that which reacts to the "me" in the ongoing internal conversation that he calls thought: "The 'I' reacts to the self which arises through the taking of the attitudes of others. Through taking those attitudes we have introduced the 'me' and we react to it as an 'I.'"[14] The great complication of the "I," however, is that although it definitely exists, it is also entirely elusive. The "I" is outside language and therefore can never be adequately represented or fully known—as soon as it is taken into language it becomes only another version of the "me." If the self consisted only of the "me," then it would be predictable and knowable, but, as it is, the presence of the "I" means for Mead that it is neither. Because of the existence of the "I," the self as a "whole" is permanently elusive: "It is because of the 'I' that we say that we are never fully aware of what we are, that we surprise ourselves by our own action."[15]

Mead, like Ford, is rejecting the idea of the self as isolated or independent in a Cartesian sense, but, at the same time, he is also rejecting any full-blown form of social or cultural determinism in which the self is simply or entirely a product of external forces or (in a more postmodern vein) of language: the "I" for Mead remains vital (on an individual and social level) and intangible. In keeping with Mead's account of the "I," Ford emphasizes several times in "Charity" the sheer mysteriousness of Nancy's newly emerging self. Her confusion in the passage quoted earlier ("What was that thing she was?"), her sense that what she is becoming is beyond or outside language is repeated rather than resolved at the end of the story. In the following passage, for example, a sentimentalized epiphany in which her new self is articulable is replaced by one—implicitly more real but explicitly much more tentative—where it isn't:

> Inside the enclosed room a strange, otherworldly golden glow seemed to fall on everything now. On Tom. On her own hands and arms. On the

> bed. All through the static air, like a fog. It was beautiful, and for a moment she wanted to speak to Tom, to wake him, to tell him that something or other would be all right, just as he'd hoped; to be enthusiastic in some hopeful and time-proven way. But she didn't and then the golden fog disappeared, and for an instant she seemed to understand *slightly* better the person she was—though she lacked a proper word for it, and knew only that the time for saying so many things was over. (*MS*, 216–17)

Yet on the other hand, as Mead argues and as Nancy's encounter with the tourists suggests, this mysterious, intangible "I" does not and cannot exist separately from a more straightforward socially constituted "me." In "Charity," in fact, the "I" seems to emerge as a gap in this socially constituted self, a gap that would clearly not be apparent if that self did not already itself exist. Late in the story, while watching TV in her hotel room, Nancy remembers going to baseball games with her father when she was a child but realizes that her memories are only partial—she remembers some things but not others. These partial memories are then linked to the partial understanding of the tourists on the bus. To remember one's own life but not remember it *fully* is like being observed by another person but not being *fully* understood by that person. Both experiences feel liberating because of, rather than in spite of, their incompleteness, "though the attempt at memory made her feel better—more settled in the same singular, getting-on-with-it way that standing on the sunny street being misidentified by a busload of Japanese tourists had made her feel: as if she was especially credible when seen without the benefit of circumstance and the encumbrances of love, residues of decisions made long, long ago" (*MS*, 215). We may say, then, based on the above, that Ford's pragmatic version of selfhood, like Mead's, consists of an interplay of remembering and forgetting, understanding and misunderstanding, convention and novelty in which both terms are required and neither is given priority. This self is neither fixed (like the Cartesian or rational self) nor ungrounded or decentered (like certain versions of the postmodern self).

At the climax of "Charity," Nancy, having decided that her marriage to Tom is over, notices a young man in a wheelchair playing with his daughter on the grass outside her motel room: "An ex-jock, she thought. A shallow-end diving accident, or some football collision that left him flying his kite from a metal chair. A pity" (*MS*, 218). She steps outside to observe their game and then, in the story's concluding paragraphs, is invited to play along:

> "Do you want to fly our kite?" the man was saying to her, his voice trailing up at the end, almost like Tom's. He was, for some reason, smiling now, his eyes bright, looking back over his hairy round shoulder with a new attitude. . . . The kite, its silky monofilament bellying upward in a long sweep, danced on the wind almost out of sight, a fleck upon the eye.
>
> "Oh do, do," the little girl called out. "It'll be so good." She had her arms spread wide and up over her head, as if measuring some inconceivable wish. She was permanently smiling.
>
> "Yes," Nancy said, walking toward them. "Of course." (*MS*, 219)

This is, by some distance, the most cheerful scene in the whole of *A Multitude of Sins*, and one of its intentions is clearly to offer a rare image of happiness and possibility amidst the more general gloom and disarray. In order to achieve this, however, the scene must revisit and revise the image of the fragmented body that looms so large in "Quality Time" and "Abyss." If the deaths of Frances Bilandic and the unnamed pedestrian imply that the only alternative to the shallowness and incoherence of postmodern selfhood is a kind of physical disintegration, the young man's disability suggests with an audacious (possibly disturbing) literalness the possibility of a viable third state, a position between the false perfection of the postmodern image and complete disintegration. Ford's pragmatic position is, in this scene, being symbolically articulated via the young man's damaged, partial, but still very much functioning body. He is a physical manifestation of the pragmatic idea of truth occupying a messy but livable middle ground—neither the fantasy of perfection nor the nightmare of dispersal, but always something in-between.

If these concluding symbolic connections feel a little strange, even possibly a little strained, it testifies, I would suggest, to both the seriousness and the difficulty of Ford's efforts to find and dramatize a viable realist alternative to the possibilities offered by a bipolar postmodernism. It would be wrong to imply that Ford in *A Multitude of Sins* or elsewhere discovers or develops a fully worked out answer to the postmodern situation he finds himself in. Ford is offering us, at most, a set of concerns and the possibility of an alternative, more pragmatic way of thinking. Whether similar concerns and possibilities exist in the work of other contemporary American novelists is a question that lies, unfortunately, beyond the scope of this study, but if they do, then my arguments here may well have some broader uses. Rather than being merely postmodernism's crudely representational, deterministic, or essentialist Other, Ford's work raises the possibility that contemporary realism may, to the extent that it aligns itself with the lessons of pragmatism, offer a plausible and sophisticated corrective to postmodernism's relativizing or dehumanizing tendencies. Understood and practiced in this way, realism can acknowledge the always constructed nature of "the real" while at the same time staying alert to the ethical difficulties and confusions that such a recognition, if understood too loosely or taken too far, is always likely to produce. How exactly it can do this without reverting to some more metaphysical notion of the true or real remains an open question to be engaged with differently by different writers. William James in 1907 famously noted that pragmatism was a method rather than a doctrine: "It lies in the midst of our theories," he suggested, "like a corridor in a hotel. Innumerable chambers open out of it."[16] Ford's efforts in *A Multitude of Sins* and especially in "Charity," which emphasize, after Mead, the relational, communal nature of truth and self making, indicate one path that a pragmatic realism might take, but there will be, necessarily, many others.

FIVE

"Everything Good Is on the Highway"

Permanence and Transition in *The Lay of the Land*

At the end of part 1 of *The Lay of the Land*, Frank Bascombe recalls, in paraphrase, one of Emerson's most famous axioms: "Still, old Emerson says, power resides in shooting the gulf, in darting to an aim. The soul becomes. My soul, though, has become tired of this day" (*LL*, 200). This idea of power abiding not in static states or in the concepts and abstractions that are the intellectual equivalent of such places but rather in the movement between, away, or toward them is key to Emerson's philosophy, and this particular phrase from "Self-Reliance" has been frequently referred to, especially by literary neopragmatists, as the cornerstone of Emerson's thought and consequently of the American pragmatist tradition that he founded. Unparaphrased, the quotation runs: "Power ceases in the instant of repose; it resides in the moment of transition from a past to a new state, in the shooting of the gulf, in the darting to an aim."[1] In *Independence Day* Frank thinks of the same lines while en route to Cooperstown with Paul and wishes that his son would take them to heart: "In my official view, absolutely nothing should be missed from here on, geography offering a natural corroboration to Emerson's view that power resides in moments of transition, in 'shooting the gulf, in darting to an aim.' Paul could do himself a heap of good to set aside his *New Yorker* and try contemplating his own status in these useful terms: transition, jettisoning the past. 'Life only avails, not having lived'" (*ID*, 286).

In *Independence Day* the necessary transition finally comes in the negative form of Paul's injury—it is only that which changes things. The earlier novel in that sense, as I have argued, tests the limits of pragmatism but stays within its overall logic—the logic that suggests that abandoning the past and moving forward to a different, more open future is the best way to live. In *The Lay of the Land*, the situation is somewhat different. Frank's offhand acknowledgment that his soul has "become tired" points to a much larger sense of disillusionment and doubt—if *Independence Day* tested the limits of pragmatism, then *The Lay of the Land* frequently appears to want to reject it altogether. The clearest evidence of these antipragmatic urges is Frank's attachment through the bulk of the novel to the philosophy of what he calls the "Permanent Period." The Permanent Period has three major characteristics: an emphasis on living in the present without worrying or thinking much about either the past or the future; a desire to locate and inhabit a solid, fixed character; and a consequent wish to give up the process of becoming in favor of simply being. Frank states and restates these values energetically and frequently over the course of the novel. To give just one example from the second chapter: "[The Permanent Period] portended an end to perpetual becoming, to thinking that life schemed wonderful changes for me, even if it didn't. It portended a blunt break with the past and provided a license to think of the past only indistinctly. . . . It portended that I say to myself and mean it, even if I thought I said it every day and already really meant it: 'This is how the shit I *am*. My life is *this* way'" (*LL*, 54). Frank discovers or invents the Permanent Period, he tells us, in direct response to the craziness of the Haddam real estate boom of the early 1990s, when the market "went nuts" and "expectations left all breatheable atmosphere behind" (*LL*, 84). Looking back on this period, Frank remembers feeling that "a malign force seemed to be in full control of every bit of real property on the seaboard, and possibly farther away. Possibly everywhere. . . . And this force, I realized, was the economy" (*LL*, 85). The previously positive and mutually supportive relationship that existed (in Frank's mind at least) between ideas of Emersonian self-creation and the practices of the American free market has disappeared. Instead of encouraging happiness and hopefulness, as it previously seemed to, the real estate business has begun to threaten those same values:

> Something had hardened in Haddam, so that having a decent house on a safe street, with like-minded neighbors and can't-miss equity growth—a home as a natural extension of what was wanted from life, a sort of minor-league Manifest Destiny—all that now seemed to piss people off,

> instead of making them ecstatic. . . . The redemptive theme in the civic drama had been lost. And realty itself—stage manager to that drama—had stopped signaling our faith in the future, our determination not to give in to dread, our blitheness in the face of life's epochal slowdown. (*LL*, 90)

Change has become less attractive to Frank, then, because it has become associated with a particularly unappealing set of socioeconomic tendencies. Optimism has mutated into greed, and in this context, conservatism becomes (paradoxically perhaps) a liberal value. Although Frank is not exactly an environmentalist, his doubts about Tom Benivalle's development plans indicate a similar set of political and philosophical anxieties: "Flattening pretty cornfields for seven-figure mega-mansions isn't, after all, really *helping* people in the way that assisting them to find to find a modest home they want—and that's already there—helps them" (*LL*, 198).

If the values of the Permanent Period are born from a particular economic situation and a consequent crisis of conscience, they are reinforced by other, more elemental and individual events. Frank's marriage to Sally Caldwell is imagined as a perfect expression of Permanent Period principles ("we de-emphasized becoming in behalf of being. We permanently renounced melancholy and nostalgia" [*LL*, 230]), but before the novel opens its apparent sureties have been catastrophically undermined by the reappearance of Sally's first husband, Wally, whom everyone had long assumed to be dead. Wally's reappearance and Sally's decision to leave Frank to be with him are explicitly associated with contingency, but contingency of the worst, most unlucky kind: "I understood she'd just come unexpectedly face-to-face with *big contingency*—the thing we'd schemed against and almost beaten" (*LL*, 231). Adding to Frank's woes, and posing another threat to the Permanent Period, is the fact that subsequent to Sally's departure he has been diagnosed with prostate cancer and is now walking around with radioactive titanium pellets in his groin. As a result of this cancer, when Frank thinks of death in *The Lay of the Land* he thinks not only, as in the previous Bascombe novels, of Ralph's death, located in the past, but also of his own death, located at some uncertain point in the future.

Although the Permanent Period is in most ways diametrically opposed to the Emersonian values of movement and transition and to the associated notion of becoming, when placed, as it is, in opposition to cancer, divorce, and untrammeled capitalist expansionism it may seem, and is surely intended to seem, both appealing and sensible.[2] If the past is characterized as a place of error and regret and the future is imagined as a place of decline, uncertainty, and/or death, then it is not surprising that Frank prefers to live in a persistent, permanent present where both these forms of threat can be avoided. Although he acknowledges at certain points that the Permanent Period may have its weaknesses or blind spots, overall through the first three-quarters of the novel it is presented, I would argue, as a plausible and admirable way of seeing and living in the world.

What is more, when the Permanent Period is finally abandoned, as it is in the scene in the Manasquan Bar at the end of part 3, it is, importantly and tellingly, not abandoned in favor of an Emersonian alternative. Rather, it is replaced by the even more insistently metaphysical notion of "Acceptance." The problem with permanence from the perspective of acceptance is that it is not as final or conclusive as it needs or promises to be. It relies, even though it pretends not to, on mutability and change, when what is actually needed is the truth. The problem with permanence, in other words, is that it is just not permanent enough:

> *That* was my lie, my big fear, the great pain I couldn't fathom even the thought of surviving, and so didn't fathom it; fathomed instead life as a series of lives, variations on a theme that sheltered me. The lie being: It's not Ralph's death that's woven into everything like a secret key, it's his *not death*, the *not* permanence—the extra beat awaited, the mutability of every fact, the grinning eyebrows-raised chance that something's waiting even if it's not. These were my sly ruses and slick tricks, my surface intrigues and wire-pulls, all played *against* permanence, not *to* it. (*LL*, 357)

The scene in the Manasquan Bar, is, in this sense, a false climax. It appears to offer itself as a revelation of a new viewpoint and a reversal of an old one, but it actually only reinforces, using a slightly different terminology, the same values that have been promulgated throughout.

On the surface, then, *The Lay of the Land* steps away from the pragmatic ideas and values discovered and explored in the previous two Bascombe novels and seeks to replace them with something a lot more conservative and quietistic. Although the meaning of "Acceptance" is not always consistent, the term, as used by Frank, usually suggests a strong desire for stasis and for the avoidance of confusion, complication, or uncertainty. Looking forward to his Thanksgiving dinner, he notes, for example: "What I desire . . . is that the freshening spirit of acceptance render today free of significant pretexts, contexts, subtexts—texts of any kind; be just a day when I'm not the theme, the constant, not expected to make things better" (*LL*, 366–67). Frank's desire here to avoid "texts of any kind" clearly contradicts his belief in *Independence Day* that everything is made of words—it suggests, to use the language of contemporary theory, a rather literal, and quite unpragmatic, wish to find a place outside discourse. That the appeal of such a location is primarily metaphysical is suggested by Frank's quasi-spiritual musings near the end of the novel after he has recovered from being shot in the chest by teenage criminals. At this point the novel, which has previously maintained a flirtatious but primarily ironic relationship to Tibetan Buddhism via the presence of Frank's partner, Mike Mahoney (aka Lobsang Dhargey), becomes distinctly New Age: "The best motivational question in the spirituality catechism, and one seeking an answer worth remembering, may *not* be 'Am I good?' . . . but 'Do I have a heart at all?' Do I see good as even a possibility? The Dalai Lama in *The Road to the Open Heart* argues I definitely do. And I can say I think I do, too. But anymore—as they say back down in New Jersey—anymore than that is more spiritual than I can get" (*LL*, 476).

Kathy Knapp argues that this passage should be taken at face value and that it indeed contains the novel's main ethical conclusions, and it is certainly the case that the novel appears to throw its weight behind these ideas.[3] That it does so is evidenced in particular by the fact that the passage just quoted is preceded by a paragraph in which Frank quotes the same lines from Saint Paul and Wallace Stevens that Ford himself has often quoted in interviews when asked to explain his views on religion or the moral purposes of art.[4] There is a real sense, in other words, that Frank's concluding, distinctly fatalistic statements of acceptance—"at a certain point around the course, can you do much to change your chances? Isn't it really more a matter of readying? Of life as prelude?" (*LL*, 477)—bear its author's stamp of approval and that, since this is the end of the trilogy, this may really be offered as Ford's final word.

I want to argue now and in the remainder of this chapter, however, that there is another, very different, even contradictory (but equally, if not more, convincing) way of reading *The Lay of the Land*, one that retrieves from the margins or interstices of the text the pragmatic Emersonian values that Frank's persistent concern with the conceptual abstractions of the Permanent Period, Acceptance, the Next Level, and so on encourages us, it may seem, either to forget about or to reimagine as naive and/or threatening. In order to begin this alternative reading, we need to go back to Emerson's notions of power, repose, and transition and relate them in a quite direct way to the structure of the novel. When Emerson talks about transition in the famous lines from "Self-Reliance" he is usually understood as meaning the transition between *ideas* or, more specifically, between metaphors or even words, but the term may also have a more literal, even material suggestiveness.[5] Jonathan Levin, in his book-length study of the metaphor of transition, quotes from Emerson's essay on Plato where Emerson suggests that the "experience of poetic creativeness" is "not found in staying at home, nor yet in travelling, but in transitions from one to the other, which must therefore be adroitly managed to present as much transitional surface as possible."[6] Levin then goes on to comment: "Staying at home appears to describe a state of complete familiarity; travelling, by contrast, suggests a pure exoticism. . . . Transition should instead bring the familiar into contact with the unknown, a process that extends knowledge further into the mysterious margin of things, even as it defamiliarises the very categories through which that movement is conducted."[7] Understood like this, transition appears connected to physical and to intellectual movement. "Home" is used primarily as a metaphor by Emerson to suggest all that is known, familiar, or customary, but Ford's emphasis on realty as a prime expression of Americanness has the effect of taking that metaphor much further and linking it much more directly to material and social experiences—people like the Markhams in *Independence Day* and Clare Suddruth in *The Lay of the Land* are seeking or refusing Emersonian self-reliance by *literally* moving (or failing to move) house. And if the metaphor of home is literalized by Ford, the metaphor of transition I would argue is also. In the Bascombe trilogy the mental or emotional movements that Emerson recommends are hardly thinkable apart from instances of physical movement—in *Independence Day* we might think, among numerous examples, of Frank's road trip with Paul or of his encounter with Mr. Tanks, who drives a moving truck. In both *Independence Day* and *The Lay of the Land* Frank spends a significant amount of time abroad in his car, and it is while he is in his car, I want to argue, moving through New Jersey in a process of quite literal transition from one place or one appointment to another, that many of his most important experiences actually occur.

"Up again, old heart. Everything good is on the highway," Frank cheerfully announces at the beginning of one chapter, lifting another ringing phrase from Emerson (this time from "Experience"), but then immediately adds, "In this instance, New Jersey Route 35, the wide mercantile Pike up Barnegat Neck" (*LL*, 266). Emerson's intellectual or spiritual highway is thus wittily actualized as a specific stretch of asphalt, a gesture that may seem crude or even possibly ironic but is actually in perfect keeping with the intentions of the original, since in "Experience" Emerson uses "highway" both in the simple (if metaphorical) sense of a road and in the more particular sense of a route that is both direct and much used.

Frank's journeys to and fro in *The Lay of the Land*—from Sea Clift to Haddam and back again, from Sea Clift to Asbury Park and then Manasquan, and so on—may appear to be mainly or merely interludes between the much larger set pieces around which the novel is constructed, instances of fictional and psychological downtime before the more important events begin. I want to argue, however, in opposition to this certainly not unreasonable way of thinking, that these intervals are actually crucial and that they should be read not as digressions or necessary pauses but as quite direct instances of Emersonian transition, of the "shooting of the gulf." In order to understand how they function as such, it is important to consider them in relation to the scenes that they serve to connect. We may (to tweak the metaphor again) think of movement or transition in this sense not only as both intellectual and literal but also as *formal* in the literary sense—a movement or transition within the narrative between different instances of the relatively fixed or stable element of the scene.[8]

There are nine major scenes in *The Lay of the Land*. The first of these is Frank and Mike's meeting with Tom Benivalle, and the last is the scene on Timbuktu Street where Frank spectacularly fails to sell a house to the very willing Mr. Bagosh. The content of these scenes is varied, even eclectic, and they certainly do not connect causally in order to form a tightly focused or directed plot. (The disconnected, dispersed quality of these nine major scenes is in large part responsible for the digressive, rather plotless feel of the novel as a whole.) They are, however, thematically linked—similar concerns recur but in different forms. The idea of death, disintegration, or impermanence, for example, is strongly present in Frank's visit to the funeral home to pay his respects to Ernie McAuliffe and in his meetings with Clare Suddruth and Wade Arcenault. It also plays a major part in his epiphany in the Manasquan Bar.[9] Similarly, the novel's concerns about the deteriorating condition of America are explored via Frank's meeting with Tom Benivalle, the political conversations in the Johnny Appleseed Bar, and his discussion with Clare Suddruth about "normality." As these examples suggest, the main purpose of all these scenes is to support and further develop the particular set of concerns (about death, the self, and America) that feeds Frank's attachment to the Permanent Period. The main set pieces of the novel, in other words, serve mainly to reinforce Frank's anxieties about temporariness and the waning of national and personal identity and values and therefore to reinforce his belief (encapsulated in the Permanent Period) that the best way to respond to current conditions is to seek, even if belatedly, a measure of metaphysical certainty.

The most striking example of the philosophical and political implications of these set-piece sections occurs when Frank meets Clare Suddruth, Vietnam veteran and plumbing contractor, and attempts to sell him a large and expensive house on the beach in Sea Clift. When they meet, rather than going into the house, Clare takes Frank around to the front and shows him several cracks in the concrete piers, which are designed to stop the house being blown or washed away. This, after Frank's initial shock has dissipated, leads the two men into a broad and "quasi-philosophical" discussion of the whole idea of foundations and in particular (by implication) the moral foundations of America. Clare fervently wants to believe, he tells Frank, that nothing "could happen in this country to make *normal* just not be possible," but he can't quite manage to believe it: "'But I *want* to believe it. And *that's* what scares the shit right out of me. And don't think they're not sitting over there in those other countries that hate us licking their chops at what they see us doing over here, fucking around trying to decide which of these dopes to make President. You think these people here'—a toss of the Clare Suddruth head toward crumbling

61 Surf Road—'have foundation problems? *We've* got foundation problems'" (*LL*, 283).

Given that the novel was published in 2006 and is set in 2000, there can be little doubt that the unspoken context of these discussions is the terrorist attacks of September 11, 2001, and that the scene suggests that Ford's turn toward foundationalism (as opposed to the antifoundationalism of the Emersonian and pragmatic tradition) is in part a response to the national trauma of 9/11—in part a desire to discover a kind of certainty in the aftermath of an event that created a great deal of uncertainty and fear. The scene in the Johnny Appleseed Bar in which Frank gets into an argument about the presidential election and is assaulted by a drunken George W. Bush supporter suggests a similar set of anxieties about the weakness and disorderliness of the American body politic. All of this prefiguring serves to reinforce our sense (and Frank's sense) that the concerns that prompted the Permanent Period are real and pressing and to indicate that the main dramatic question the novel is asking, the main conflict it is dramatizing, is whether or not the Permanent Period is strong and convincing enough as an idea to hold out against the various forces that are arrayed against it.

The novel, understood in this sense, is staging an updated version of the antique struggle between chaos and order, formlessness and form, with the Permanent Period being what Frank Kermode has called a useful fiction—a concept that, even if not entirely believed in, can offer a humanly necessary sense of organization and meaning.[10] The Permanent Period, in other words, is not only a term that *describes* Frank's efforts to control his fears, it is also itself, as an idea, a major element *of* those efforts—it is a concept that abstracts and thus tames the variety and disorderliness of Frank's experience. Frank himself ironically hints at that function when he suggests that the way to get over the kind of fears Clare is experiencing is to "accept the Permanent Period as your personal savior" (*LL*, 284).

There is, however, as I have already suggested, another quite different way of formulating this novel's major concerns. Rather than life being understood as an attempt to control and order disorderly experience via concepts, it can be understood in more Emersonian terms as being defined by the fluid, exhilarating, uncertain movement *between* concepts. After his meeting with Clare

Suddruth, Frank gets back into his car and drives to Asbury Park to meet Wade Arcenault and watch with him the demolition of the Queen Regent Hotel. The meeting with Wade proves to be a recapitulation (albeit rather different in tone) of the concerns about impermanence and decay suggested by his meeting with Clare Suddruth. Between these two events, however, on the literal and metaphorical highway, Frank's experience is very different: "I love this post-showing interlude in the car. . . . It's the *moment d'or* which the Shore facilitates perfectly, offering exposure to the commercial-ethnic-residential zeitgeist of a complex republic, yet shelter from most of the ways the republic gives me the willies" (*LL*, 289). The highway offers a shelter from fear and self-doubt but not, crucially, from complexity, the unknown, or the uncertain. In fact, what the highway seems to offer is the possibility of such qualities becoming interesting and enlivening rather than frightening. This kind of movement is not an example of traveling in the pejorative sense that Emerson understands that term—which is to say, it is not the expression of a desire, motivated by a lack of proper self-trust, to embrace some supposedly higher or better reality. When Emerson criticizes travel, as he does at some length in "Self-Reliance," his criticism is rooted in a kind of mid-nineteenth-century intellectual patriotism. He believes America as a culture and landscape is rich enough and contains sufficient possibility and openness to fuel or fund the spontaneous, self-reliant leaps that he is proposing.[11] It is a faith that Frank, in an updated form, appears to share: "I count it a good day when I can keep *all* things that give me the willies out of my thinking, and in their places substitute vistas I can appreciate, even unwittingly. Which is why I take the scenic route now, and why when I get restless I fly out to Moline or Flint or Fort Wayne for just a few hours' visit—since there I can experience the new and the complex, coupled with the entirely benign and knowable" (*LL*, 289).

The coupling of the "new and complex" with the "benign and knowable" (especially when it takes place within the decidedly American context of the Midwest) is surely a good definition of what Emerson means by transition. Such successful moments, however, as both Frank and Emerson recognize, are always temporary and hemmed in by limitations. Frank's *moment d'or* is halted after only a paragraph by a sudden, out-of-the-blue set of thoughts about his experience of being diagnosed with cancer. After such an experience, Frank tells us, the challenge becomes "how, post-op, to maintain a supportable existence that resembles an actual life, instead of walking the windy, trash-strewn streets in a smudged sandwich board that shouts IMPAIRED!" (*LL*, 290). Such feelings are a particularly intense version of what Emerson calls self-doubt, a form of weakness or misunderstanding that in turn leads the sufferer to take refuge in imitation. If we cannot find meaning, value, and interest in ourselves or, by extension, in the ordinary environment in which we live ("the society of your contemporaries, the connection of events"), then, Emerson suggests, we will be led to seek them outside in some external and preexisting creed.[12] Such imitation, he notes, is "suicide," and Frank's reaction to feeling impaired is indeed to attach himself directly, if paradoxically, to *death* as a form of consolation and surety. After noting that being diagnosed with cancer destroys "*all* good feeling" and creates a sense of meaninglessness, he then goes on to suggest that in such circumstances death itself can become something one can rely on and that it can even become the object of a strange kind of desire. The relevant passage (quoted below) is remarkable in that it indicates both (1) that the fear of personal extinction leads Frank away from the highway and toward the search for metaphysical certainty but also (2) that the metaphysical certainty he reaches for is itself (as Emerson suggests it must be) quite explicitly deathly. It is a foundationalist gesture, in other words, that contains not far below the surface an antifoundationalist response:

> And I'll also admit that in the highly discretionary lives most of us lead, there *is* sweet satisfaction to this being *it*, and not having *it* always out there to dread. . . . This longing for satisfaction, I believe, is in the hearts of those strange Korea vets who admit to wartime atrocities they never committed and never would've. . . . There *is* a desire to face some music, even if it's a tune played only in your head—a desire for the real, the permanent, for a break in the clouds that tells you, This is how you are and will always be. (*LL*, 290–91)

The desire to fix one's character, as the Permanent Period suggests is necessary, the desire to "be" rather than "become," is in fact, this passage implies, closely connected to the desire to be dead. If we think of living as an ongoing, time-bound process rather than a fixable or definable "thing," then this connection between metaphysical certainty and death makes perfect sense. To think of life in that way, however, is to adopt the Emersonian perspective, which in *The Lay of the Land* occurs only intermittently and when it does occur tends (as in the section just discussed) to quickly dissipate and be replaced by the conceptualizing logic of permanence.

It is hard sometimes not to sense a measure of unjustified gloom and disillusionment, even crankiness, in the way the novel plays out these maneuvers. Early on in the novel, for example, in one of its liveliest passages, Frank takes to the road, declaring with Emersonian optimism: "Surface roads are never a pain in the ass, no matter where we roam. And I'm always interested in what's new, what's abandoned, what's in the offing, what will never be" (*LL*, 24). What follows is a brief, exhilarating, enlivening, Whitmanesque tour through the mishmash of backroads New Jersey—a grubby, antipastoral landscape that speaks comically of the variety and incompatibility of human desires:

> At the turn-off for Collier's Mills Wildlife Management Area, a billboard proclaims a WILD WEST CITY—MASTODON EXHIBIT AND WATERSLIDE. A few cars, dust-caked green Plymouths and a rusted-out Chevy Nova with white shoe-polish 4-$ales on their windshields, sit on the dry shoulder at the woods' edge. One lonely-guy sex shop lurks back in the trees with a blinking red-and-yellow roof sign, awaiting whoever's out here to abandon his pet but finds himself in the mood for some nasty. The White Citizen's Action Alliance has "adopted" the highway. The only car we pass is an Army Humvee driven by a soldier in a helmet and a camo suit. (*LL*, 24)

Such passages offer an updated, Americanized version of the unconceptualized Bergsonian flow that William James saw as an important complement to pragmatism. For James, after Henri Bergson, the important thing for the philosopher is to enter into the "living, moving, active thickness of the real," the "conflux of the same with the different," and to avoid as much as possible the intellectualist tendency to dissect and explain.[13] As he writes in *A Pluralistic Universe*: "Reality *falls* in passing into conceptual analysis; it *mounts* in living its own undivided life—it buds and bourgeons, changes and creates. . . . Philosophy should seek this kind of living understanding of the movement of reality, not follow science in vainly patching together fragments of its dead results."[14] Frank's immersion in the flux is, however (as in the previous example), only temporary, and its implications are easily reversible. About thirty pages after his trip along Route 37 Frank remembers that landscape in a way that seems specifically designed to squash its Bergsonian and Emersonian implications. He asks himself suddenly, "What would real scientists, decades on, say about us here on our own patch of suburban real estate" (*LL*, 45), and, after a few mundane and comical suggestions, concludes more seriously that their most striking discovery would be how deeply unoriginal and uninventive contemporary American culture is and, moreover, that if contemporary Americans even *think* about doing something "outside" the box they immediately realize that they risk "desolation and the world looking at us with menace" (*LL*, 46) and so give up the attempt. A more complete reversal of the Emersonian ideal of America is hard to imagine—not only has Frank, via his imaginary scientists, entirely conceptualized and thus fixed the transitional, fluid nature of experience, he has also concluded that Americans are not bold nonconformists displaying the careless "nonchalance of boys who are sure of a dinner" but are cowardly conventionalists worried above all what other people might think of them.[15]

That there are specific, identifiable reasons for this abandonment of pragmatic principles Frank openly admits—he offers prostate cancer and his anxieties about "our present and very odd state of human development" as reasons why he might be feeling the way he is. But the fact that he recognizes the very specific and contingent causes of his disillusionment doesn't stop him from feeling disillusioned anyway. He is caught, we might say, in two minds, and the novel as a result is caught in two minds also. I have given two examples of the way it attaches and then detaches itself from an Emersonian perspective, but I could give many more. It is a novel that, in this way, frequently seems to contradict or misremember itself, asserting at one moment the importance of becoming and at the next the importance of being. Interlude follows scene and vice versa in a repeating pattern of thesis and antithesis.

If the novel operates throughout, as I have been suggesting, on these two distinct but contradictory levels, undercutting and second-guessing itself as it moves along, then the final question is clearly: How, if at all, does the novel resolve this duality by the end? In the previous two Bascombe novels a moment of crisis in which a dominant metaphor is overturned is followed by a conclusion in which an alternative, more comprehensive or useful metaphor is offered in its place. In *The Sportswriter* the final consolatory image is literary (the symbol of invisibility and all that it portends), and in *Independence Day* it is social (Frank's reconciliation with Sally and his merging with the Fourth of July crowds). This same pattern is broadly present in *The Lay of the Land*, but the final consolatory image is, perhaps more surprisingly, medical.

The very final paragraph of *The Lay of the Land* appears to echo the concluding lines of *Independence Day*. As Frank and Sally's plane makes its descent into Rochester, Minnesota, home of the Mayo Clinic, there is a sense of them rejoining a human community, reentering life understood as the actual rather than the merely desired or imagined. It is the end of the journey, the end of an interlude, which may suggest, judging by the way other interludes in the novel have ended, a reassertion of the values of permanence over those of transition, yet that is not quite the case here. Frank has just informed us of his decision to leave his body to science when he dies rather than having his ashes scattered at sea, as he previously planned. Like his similar decision at the end of *Independence Day* to be buried in Cut Off, Louisiana, rather than at home in Haddam near Ralph, this clearly signals a shaking off of his fear of loss and a willingness to move more positively and hopefully forward: "The medical kids, I felt, would treat me with all the dignity and compassion I'm due and no doubt with a measure of irreverence and amusement, which seemed right and a better way to turn a small event—my death and life—into a slightly less small one, while keeping things simple and still making a contribution" (*LL*, 485). Medicine, in other words, stands in this instance for a benign, down-to-earth form of progress—the same kind of values that realty used to represent for Frank but doesn't anymore. But medicine is not only or primarily progressive, it is also, crucially, at the same time protective; in other words, it resists the future, or certain aspects of the future, at the same time as it moves forward into it. When Frank describes the Mayo Clinic from the air it is revealed as a symbolic, if slightly surreal, solution to all the varied problems of personal transitoriness and national weakness and disorder that the Permanent Period previously seemed best placed to counter: "Settlement's thickening and widening to include vacant baseball diamonds, a Guard armory with starred tanks and trucks out back (in case the fuckers make it this far inland, and they might), the Applebee's, the red blinking tower of an old AM transmitter morphed now into all new radiography—cell phone, cable, radar, NORAD, government surveillance. I don't yet see the great Mayo citadel with its own antennas and helipads, ICBM launchers and surface-to-air missiles to shoot down marauding microbes, but it's there" (*LL*, 484).

Although the novel ends nine months prior to 9/11, this image of the Mayo equipped with missiles designed to shoot down "marauding microbes" indicates a merging in Frank's mind of the internal, biological threats to his own body and the broader, external, political and military threats to the body politic of the United States. Medical science, represented here by a blending of military and medical technology, appears to offer Frank, in contrast to the abstraction and metaphysics of the Permanent Period, a more direct, practical, and effective way of dealing with his various personal and political fears. If, as Frank admits in one of his more Emersonian moods, the Permanent Period is flawed because "it's loony . . . to think that by lowering expectations and keeping ambitions to a minimum we can ever avert the surprising and the unwanted" (*LL*, 189), then the image of the heavily armed Mayo Clinic suggests that a better, more optimistic way of responding to such threats, rather than seeking to merely avoid or avert them, is to face them head-on, to, in some sense, confront them and shoot them down.

It is an unsettling way to conclude, perhaps—paranoid in its way, even faintly xenophobic—and one that, for that reason, should not be taken too literally, yet it does remind us usefully of Ford's occasional realist impatience with idealism and the vagaries of mere thought or language. The same impetus that leads him in *A Multitude of Sins* to seek the damaged or dying human body as an alternative to the thinness and superficiality of postmodern experience leads him at the end of this novel to (rather more positively) identify the Mayo Clinic, where bodies are repaired and maintained, as a place of ultimate safety: "These buildings, I thought, could take good care of anybody" (*LL*, 168). Such an emphasis on the possibilities of applied science, although out of keeping with many recent readings of pragmatism, is not necessarily antipragmatic. John Dewey, for example, directly associates pragmatism with the scientific method and contrasts the in-built modesty of experimentation with what he sees as the traditional hubris of philosophy:

> "One might say that the profuseness of attestations to supreme devotion to the truth on the part of philosophy is matter to arouse suspicion. For it has usually been a preliminary to the claim of being a peculiar organ of

access to highest and ultimate truth. Such it is not. . . . Truth is a collection of truths; and these constituent truths are in the keeping of the best available methods of enquiry and testing as to matters-of-fact; methods which are, when collected under a single name, science."[16]

Ford, of course, is a novelist rather than a philosopher or a scientist, but as a *realist* novelist he is perhaps more committed than some to a sense of a world that, like Dewey's, contains human thought and desire but cannot be contained or controlled by them. And if the body and its frailties are his favored means for emphasizing the limitations of the mind, then medicine as an application of the mind to the weaknesses of the body for the purposes of temporary but welcome improvement makes a useful final image of the kind of options and hope that Ford imagines are available.

"We thrive by casualties," Emerson puns in "Experience," an essay that Frank quotes twice in *The Lay of the Land*: "Our chief experiences have been casual."[17] And that we should seek to be casual about our own inevitable casualties is perhaps Ford's final implication. Frank's gunshot wounds, like his prostate cancer, are, once the initial excitement is over, treated with remarkable, perhaps implausible, ease and success—the doctors are cheerful and efficient, the paramedics skilled and strangely jaunty. Ford is not suggesting finally, of course, that death can be evaded or survived (although the novel's persistent low-level interest in reincarnation hints playfully at that possibility), but he is suggesting that it can be happily and pleasantly postponed, at least for a while. We end, in other words, as is usual for Ford, with the idea of moderation, of a middle way between extremes of fearfulness and hope. Such a compromise is Emersonian if we read Emerson in the way I suggested we might in the introduction, that is, as a realist. When Emerson declares in "Experience" that "everything good is on the highway," he then goes on: "The middle region of our being is the temperate zone. We may climb into the thin and cold realm of pure geometry or lifeless science, or sink into that of sensation. Between these extremes is the equator of life, of thought, of spirit, of poetry—a narrow belt."[18] The highway is being understood not only as a place of movement or transition but also, and perhaps more importantly, as a place defined by its position in the midst of things. It is the most frequently taken and the most direct route, but it is also, paradoxically, a difficult path to stick to. This is Emerson at his most realist, as I have suggested, but it is a side of Emerson that Ford never forgets or strays too far from. Emerson's spatial metaphor of the "equator of life" as a "narrow belt" is echoed by Ford's image of "the high-wire act of normalcy"—both metaphors suggest that the kinds of compromises that may seem ordinary or even banal are actually hard-won and easy to let slip. To be normal, to occupy what Emerson calls the "mid-world," is not to be merely conventional, since the convention (in the 1840s as now) is to be dissatisfied and to wish always you were someone or somewhere else. To stay on the highway, on the other hand, is to exercise the virtue of self-trust, not to travel as a means of escape but to move alertly, responsively toward a particular, inevitable end. And if this mid-world sounds intriguingly like the middle way of certain eastern religions, Frank is careful to remind us that attaching ourselves to an exotic spiritual tradition, however sensible its doctrines, is certainly not what he is arguing for: "It wouldn't be hard to be a Buddhist," he thinks in relation to Mike Mahoney, his Tibetan, and Republican, business partner. "What's hard is to be a realist" (*LL*, 44).

CONCLUSION

Canada and the Hazards of Normality

Near the close of *Independence Day* Frank Bascombe watches four parachutists wearing Stars and Stripes jumpsuits descending onto Haddam Green as part of the Fourth of July celebrations. He enjoys this "bright and chancy spectacle" but finds himself, once they have landed, immediately scanning the sky in an attempt to identify the plane they leaped from. "As always," he explains, "this is what interests me: the jump, of course, but the hazardous place jumped *from* even more; the old safety, the ordinary and predictable" (*ID*, 437). He himself would never attempt anything like a parachute jump, he then goes on to explain, "since for me, the wire, the plane, the platform, the bridge, the trestle, the window ledge—these would preoccupy me, flatter my nerve with their own prosy hazards, greater even than the risk of brilliantly daring death" (*ID*, 438).

These passages should remind us, if we need reminding, of the importance, even the centrality, of the notion of the ordinary and normal in Ford's fiction. This emphasis is, in part, simply another, different expression of his realist tendencies—a reminder that what he is most interested in as a writer is the ordinary rather than the extraordinary, the normal rather than the abnormal. But it is also rather more than that—these passages may remind us that the normal for Ford can be equated with the real only in the pragmatic sense that both are man-made constructions that, because of their constructedness, are prone to dissolution and collapse. The places of normality named above—the wire, the trestle, the bridge—may be safe, ordinary, and predictable compared to the uncertainty of what surrounds them, but they are also explicitly hazardous in their own right. Normality for Ford, rather than being the soulless expression or imposition of a dominant ideology, is always a fragile achievement easily lost and, indeed, more often than not, defined by its painful absence rather than its stultifying (or pleasing) presence. In this sense, normality is hazardous, like a wire, or a windowsill, because it is so easy to lose one's grip or footing and topple off it.

To take the argument a step further, however, we might also note that this hazardousness is precisely, for Ford and his protagonists, what makes the ordinary so persistently interesting. Frank is not attracted to the plane or the windowsill because they are simply safe or stable (or real) places, he is attracted to them because they suggest the kind of safety that may very easily be lost or abandoned. The ordinary is defined as the place *jumped from.* It is understood and valued always in relation to its opposite. It is the edginess of normality, then, in the various senses of that term, its potential to disappear or get left behind, and the fact that its very existence implies or reminds us of its opposite that Ford emphasizes and toward which he as a writer appears most strongly drawn. "To me," Dell Parsons, the narrator of *Canada* tells us in relation to his parents' intention to rob a bank, "it's the edging closer to the point of no return that's fascinating. . . . How amazingly far normalcy extends" (*C*, 92). To "edge closer" in this sense is to begin to recognize the limited and constructed nature of the normal and to free oneself from certain kinds of fixity, but to go too far—to step or fall away from the normal completely—is to risk vanity, emptiness, or worse. This is the fate of Walter Luckett in *The Sportswriter*, of Wally Caldwell in *The Lay of the Land*, and of the postmodern solipsists in *Women with Men* and *A Multitude of Sins.* It is the fate Paul Bascombe finally avoids only by lurching to the opposite extreme and becoming a Kansas City "mainstreamer" writing captions for Hallmark, and the fate Frank flirts with in *The Sportswriter* and in *The Lay of the Land* tries via the Permanent Period to defend himself against. The concerns that feed the Permanent Period suggest that Ford's fear about what lies beyond the margins of the normal may well be intensifying in the latter part of his career, and that sense is certainly borne out by *Canada*, his most recent novel, which features in Arthur Remlinger, Dell Parsons's murderous surrogate father, by far the most extreme example of a character who has separated himself from normality and its lessons. Remlinger, with his upmarket tailoring and his entire lack of moral qualms, is a disturbing blend of Colonel Kurtz and Jay Gatsby. He is an otherworldly, almost mythical figure who takes the American desire for independence to its nihilistic, libertarian conclusion. After he committed his third murder, Remlinger, Dell tells us, had "given up on any scale he himself might've provided for himself, just as he'd given up on reason. He only did what he wanted to do, within limits he alone recognized" (*C*, 382).

Remlinger as a domestic terrorist epitomizes and underlines the worry that emerges in much milder forms elsewhere in Ford, the worry that the threats to normalcy are internal rather than external, that the Emersonian willingness to push beyond conventional limits can too easily become an inhumane disdain for what is ordinary and unremarkable. These kinds of concerns are certainly not out of keeping with the Emersonian or pragmatic tradition. Emerson insists frequently on the importance and value of the everyday, but he thinks of it almost always in relation to the opposing urge or tendency, which he assumes to be ever-present, to devalue it or leave it behind. When he writes in "Experience" that "we live amid surfaces, and the true art of life is to skate well on them," he is pointing like Ford to the temporariness and fragility of the normal, as well as to the necessity of living in it.[1] And when he notes earlier in the same essay that "objections and criticisms we have had our fill of. . . . Life is not intellectual or critical but sturdy. Its chief good is for well-mixed people who can enjoy what they find without question," he is suggesting quite strongly (although not as strongly as Ford) that the tendency to reject the merely conventional can itself easily become a trite, disdainful, and inhumane convention.[2]

Ford's strong attachment to everyday reality is rooted, then, like Emerson's, in a complex sense of its insubstantiality. This insubstantiality can be pleasing and desirable in that it suggests that social convention is much less weighty and oppressive than it may sometimes seem to be, but it is also potentially alarming in that it raises the possibility of a disorienting moral groundlessness. This, as I hope I have indicated in the preceding chapters, is the fundamental tension behind Ford's best work—the desire for freedom confronted and complicated by the fear of freedom's consequences. For Ford, there is no final solution to this conundrum—no resting point at which freedom from convention can be completely detached from the anxiety of groundlessness, or vice versa—and the role of Ford as an artist therefore is not to solve this insoluble "problem" but rather to explore and reframe it in interesting and potentially helpful ways.

In *Canada* the requirements and difficulties of such reframing are brought to the fore to a greater degree than in his other major works. It is, in important ways, a novel about the difficulties of accounting for, and making a kind of sense of, experience, and it is indirectly, therefore, also a novel about writing or art. Ford quotes, via Dell Parsons, the novel's narrator, John Ruskin's remark that "composition is the arrangement of unequal things" (*C*, 19), and the two unequal, incompatible things that Dell is required throughout the novel to arrange are precisely those just-mentioned opposites that are central to Ford's work—the continuing reality of the normal, and the continuing reality of the abnormal. This is a difficult if not baffling challenge that Dell insists more than once can be met only by the practicing of a form of negative capability in which the two seemingly incompatible truths are simultaneously held in the mind: "It's best to see our life and the activities that ended it, as two sides of one thing that have to be held in the mind simultaneously to properly understand—the side that was normal and the side that was disastrous. One so close to the other. Any different way of looking at our life threatens to disparage the crucial, rational, commonplace part we lived, the part in which everything makes sense to those on the inside—and without which none of this is worth hearing about" (*C*, 32).

If we revisit for a moment the Rortyan or Wittgensteinian language I used in chapter 2, we might say, based on the above, that the difference between normality and abnormality is the difference between a language game that is familiar, "in which everything makes sense to those on the inside," and one that is unfamiliar and that appears to be incompatible and therefore to make no sense. If this is the case, then to hold *both* truths in one's mind simultaneously—as Dell insists is both possible and necessary—equates to the pragmatic position of being conscious of a plurality of possible but not necessarily compatible versions of the world. For Rorty, this is the position occupied by the postphilosophical ironist, whereas for Ford, it is the position occupied by the realist writer or realist artist.

In *Canada* this role is associated most strongly with Florence La Blanc, Arthur Remlinger's girlfriend and an amateur painter of the Edward Hopper, "Nighthawk," school who, to Dell's surprise, paints exactly and only what she sees. When Dell wonders whether Florence knows about Arthur's murders he decides that she both does and doesn't: "My private view is that she knew about them, and at the same time didn't. She was an artist. She held opposites in her mind. So much of life fits into that category" (*C*, 389). Despite, or perhaps because of, her morally ambiguous position, Florence clearly functions as the voice of realism and thus also the voice of sanity or normality in the novel. The two morals that Dell Parsons draws from his life story at the novel's conclusion—that life is "handed to us empty" and that "what you see [is] most of what there is"—are both directly drawn from his encounters with Florence. Both these assertions are antifoundationalist and antimetaphysical. There is nothing else "out there," they suggest, prior to or outside experience, no larger "hidden or opposite" meanings, in Dell's words. Instead, truth abides only in the actual and in what we make of the actual through our ability to effectively arrange or compose our perceptions of it. He advises his high school students in Windsor, Ontario, "to look as much as possible straight at the things they can see in broad daylight" (*C*, 395–96), to see the world, in other words, as Florence sees it when she paints:

> Florence was painting in the middle of Manitoba Street. Her picture was nothing more than the view straight back past the vacant post office and a pair of broken-in houses to the backs of the commercial row where I walked and that had been alive when Partreau was a whole town. . . . I couldn't see why this would be a subject for a painting, since it was right there for anybody to see any time, and wasn't beautiful—nothing like Niagara Falls in the Frederic Church picture, or the flower arrangements my father painted with his numbers kit. (*C*, 290–91)

If *Canada* is a version of the coming-of-age novel, then what Dell learns from his youthful experiences, awful as they are, is the importance of this kind of seeing and the dangers of other less realistic or pragmatic kinds. The unadorned, broken-down reality of Partreau stands in symbolic contrast to both the dangerous and improbable fantasies of his father (who owns a jigsaw puzzle of the Frederic Church painting of Niagara Falls) and to Arthur's grandiose ideas about civilization and the natural order. Arthur's libertarian belief in "natural" or "god-given" law and his disdain for rules that are merely man-made is indeed the very opposite of the pragmatic discovery that *all* rules are man-made, and nothing is, at least in that sense, natural at all. To see like a realist is to give up on such sentimental or absolutist explanations and to replace them with a respect for the actual combined with a pluralistic ability to entertain contradictory or unequal truths. As John Dewey suggests in *Experience and Nature*, "We must go behind the refinements and elaborations of reflective experience to the gross and compulsory things of our doings, enjoyments and sufferings. . . . A common divisor is a convenience and the greatest common divisor has the greatest degree of convenience. But there is no reason for supposing that its intrinsic 'reality' or truth is greater than that of the numbers it divides."[3] Dell learns this pragmatic, pluralistic wisdom directly from Florence (who is clearly a substitute mother figure), and he later practices it and passes it on to his students as a high school teacher in Windsor, Ontario. It is Florence who, by sending Dell to live in Winnipeg with her son and daughter-in-law, directly enables him to escape his past and to escape Arthur, to go to high school, as he has dreamed of doing, and to become a Canadian. It is also Florence who most forcefully and clearly articulates a view of Canada as a more attractive and *normal* alternative to the United States: "Canada was better than America, she said, and everyone knew that—except Americans. Canada had everything America ever had, but no one was mad about it. You could be normal in Canada, and Canada would love to have me" (*C*, 324–25).

Dell's actual mother commits suicide in jail after being convicted for bank robbery, a loss that clearly recalls the concerns and methods of *Rock Springs* and *The Sportswriter* discussed in chapter 1. If the loss of the mother (literal and metaphorical) precipitates the loss of the normal and the attempt to rediscover it elsewhere in other symbols or figures, then it certainly makes sense that the realist "solution" to this dilemma should be associated with the revivification of the mother figure in the form of Florence La Blanc.

However, if we are tempted to think that Florence, and Florence's reassuring maternal Canadianness, points toward a straightforwardly happy ending, a conclusive answer to the tensions that the novel explores and feeds off, if we are tempted to think that Canada, symbolically at least, is *it*, the conclusion of *Canada*, not surprisingly perhaps, suggests we should think again. It is vital in this context to recognize the implications of where *exactly* Dell Parsons ends up living the majority of his life. Windsor, Ontario, is the southernmost city in Canada and actually forms a de facto conurbation with Detroit—Dell is, in other words, as close as he could possibly get to being in the United States without actually being there. Windsor is, to recall Ford's previous metaphor, the window ledge of Canada, the place *jumped from*—the point where it merges into something else, something very different from itself. (In the novel Windsor is a place of safety, but Detroit, just across the river, is the place where Arthur Remlinger committed his first murder.)

The specifics of this eventual location are particularly notable in the context of the novel's frequent and persistent interest in the meaning of borders and border crossings. Dell's parents and Arthur Remlinger, in acting in the ways they act, cross or transgress a number of literal and metaphorical borders. They all three go beyond socially sanctioned limits—and indeed Arthur, with his monistic belief in natural law, goes so far as to deny the reality or importance of such limits entirely: "The frontier, he said, was not a natural or logical dividing point, and didn't exist in nature, and should be done away with" (*C*, 321). More broadly, the novel itself, as I have just been arguing, is deeply concerned with the border between what is normal and what isn't, and Dell, at the end, when discussing his career as an English teacher, identifies this motif as the key to his own experience: "I teach them books that to me seem secretly about my young life—*The Heart of Darkness*, *The Great Gatsby*, *The Sheltering Sky*, *The Nick Adams Stories*, *The Mayor of Casterbridge*. A mission into the void. Abandonment. A *figure*, possibly mysterious, but finally not. . . . My conceit is always 'crossing a border'; adaptation, development from a way of living that doesn't work toward one that does. It can also be about crossing a line and never being able to come back" (*C*, 395).

As the final two sentences of this quotation suggest, "crossing a border" can actually mean two quite different things—one to do with development and optimism, the other to do with catastrophe and loss. To actually cross a border is necessarily to choose or be chosen by one option or the other, but to remain *on* or *at* the border, where Dell is finally, literally and metaphorically, located, is to be able to recognize both incompatible possibilities as equally real without conclusively settling on either. This is again, in slightly different terms, what it means to perform the high-wire act of normalcy, to be, in Ford's terms, a realist writer. The border is just another fine line, a hazardous and fascinating edge around which the realist curls his toes but from which he never finally jumps, since to do so (even if it has positive results) is to give up the endless balancing act of composition and rearrangement, of trying and trying again, which is finally, Ford suggests, for the kind of writer he is, the best and only method.

NOTES

Introduction. "This Balancing of Urgent Forces"

1. Since the contrast between realism and postmodernism is central to the argument of large sections of this book, it may be helpful at the outset to offer a brief working definition of those two crucial but notoriously slippery terms. Postmodernism, as I am using the term here, describes a set of cultural and intellectual tendencies that are linked historically to the development of a late or global capitalism and philosophically to the influence of poststructuralist thought. In both its cultural and intellectual forms, postmodernism emphasizes the priority of representation over reality. From the postmodern perspective, there is no meaningful reality outside of or prior to human efforts to represent or create meaning—what we understand as the real is always a cultural and linguistic construction. In its more extreme and relativistic manifestations (as in the work of Jean Baudrillard), this kind of postmodern thinking leads to the positing of hyperreality as a contemporary condition in which even the possibility of a preexisting reality has been lost and the world has become a self-referential play of ungrounded images. Literary realism, in contrast, emphasizes reality rather than representation. This preference can be understood pejoratively as suggesting a naive, objectivist belief in the existence of a separate external reality that it is the task of literature simply to reflect. A more sophisticated and more sympathetic understanding of realism, however—and one that I would hold to—suggests that literary realism, while recognizing that what we call reality is always culturally and linguistically mediated, also holds that some versions of reality, although not pure or perfect, are demonstrably truer (or better warranted, to use the philosophical term) than others and that it is the task of realism to identify and explore those truer versions rather than to emphasize via theme or form (as modernist or postmodernist writing often tends to) their inevitable limitations. There is a great deal more that could be said about both terms, of course (the relevant literatures are huge), but I hope these brief and necessarily partial descriptions will at least allow the reader to navigate my arguments with a little more ease.

2. Documents from the Adorno, Lukács, Brecht, Benjamin, and Bloch debates are collected in Taylor, *Aesthetics and Politics.*

3. Virginia Woolf, "Mr Bennett and Mrs Brown," in Woolf, *A Woman's Essays*, 69–87; Eliot, "*Ulysses*, Order and Myth," 243.

4. See Miller, "Narrative and History."

5. Graff, *Literature against Itself*, 137, 149.

6. Bové, review of *Literature against Itself*; Gasché, "Unscrambling Positions"; Mitchell, "Intellectual Politics"; Sprinker, "Criticism as Reaction," 4; Tompkins, "Graff against Himself"; Wilde, "Strange Displacements." For examples of Graff's response to such criticism, see "Politics, Language"; Graff, "Pseudo-Politics"; and Graff, "Humanism."

7. In the preface to the 1995 edition of *Literature against Itself*, for example, Graff softened his previously hard line by suggesting that his criticisms were better directed at "vulgarised versions of deconstruction and poststructuralism than these theories and practices at their best" (xii). And two years earlier, in "Is Reason in Trouble?," he went out of his way to defend Derrida against his conservative American critics.

8. See Roland Barthes's essays "The Discourse of History" and "The Reality Effect," in *The Rustle of Language*; and Hayden White's 1988 essay "Literary Theory and Historical Writing," in *Figural Realism*. Also of relevance here are the critiques of "classic realism" offered by Colin McCabe in his influential essay "Realism and the Cinema" and by Catherine Belsey in *Critical Practice*.

9. Joe Cleary writes in the introduction to a recent issue of *Modern Language Quarterly* devoted to "peripheral realism" that "postcolonial studies has privileged modernist-associated terms such as hybridity, polyphony, pastiche, irony, and defamiliarization rather than realist-associated conceptual categories such as historical transition, class consciousness, and totality. Ultimately, this has had a detrimental effect, since it has meant that postcolonial studies has not only often ignored postcolonial realisms but also lacked intellectual criteria by which to evaluate postcolonial modernisms and magic realisms other than those generated by or largely immanent to those modes to begin with" (265–66). For skeptical accounts of affect theory, see Leys, "The Affective Turn"; and Todd Cronan's review of *The Affect Theory Reader*.

10. See Ruth Leys's account of Caruth in *Trauma*, 266–97.

11. Rebein, *Hicks, Tribes*; Dewey, *Novels from Reagan's America*. Versions of realism have also been famously defended by Tom Wolfe, Jonathan Franzen, and James Wood (in "Human, All Too Inhuman," his 2000 critique of Zadie Smith's "hysterical realism"), but in university English departments the attachment to modernist and/or postmodernist ideas remains strong. As Samuel Cohen has cogently pointed out in *After the End of History*, Fredric Jameson's account of postmodernism as a cultural dominant in *Postmodernism* has encouraged a generation of literary critics to see realism as, at best, passé. For another excellent account of the ongoing tensions between postmodern theory and literary realism, see Matthew Beaumont's essay "Reclaiming Realism," in Beaumont, *A Concise Companion*, where Beaumont describes in convincing detail the tendency of recent literary and cultural criticism, under the influence of postmodern thought, to either ignore realism completely or to understand it as a simpleminded ideological tool.

12. Jameson, *The Political Unconscious*, 152.

13. Jameson, *The Antinomies of Realism*, 5.

14. Ibid., 184–85.

15. Ibid., 11. Aside from the little-known German writer Alexander Kluge, Jameson

appears to admit no exceptions to what he sees as the dire rule of post-Jamesian "realism after realism." But can he really mean to include in his blanket denunciation writers as varied and interesting as (for example) Alice Munro, Marilynne Robinson, John McGahern, Ian McEwan, Colm Tóibín, and Deborah Eisenberg? One is forced to wonder whether Jameson actually reads such writers, or if he simply *assumes* they must be awful based on the logic of his own historical model.

16. McGurl, *The Program Era*, 377.

17. The phrase comes from Lionel Trilling, "Art and Fortune," in Trilling, *The Liberal Imagination*, 242.

18. The intermittent and eclectic nature of Ford criticism to date suggests overall a distinct lack of certainty as to how his work may most usefully be read and contextualized. Ford has been interpreted, with varying degrees of success, as an existentialist, a writer concerned with masculinity, a postsouthern writer, and a chronicler of the suburbs in the line of John Cheever, Richard Yates, and John Updike. See Guagliardo, *Perspectives*; Bone, *The Postsouthern Sense of Place*; Armengol, *Richard Ford*; Jurca, *White Diaspora*; Knapp, "Richard Ford's Frank Bascombe Trilogy." The essays in the Guagliardo collection focus mainly on the existentialist qualities of Ford's work; Bone's book discusses Ford as a postsouthern writer; Armengol's book focuses on Ford's treatment of masculinity; and Jurca and Knapp both understand Ford as primarily a suburban novelist. It is also worth noting Brian Duffy's monograph on Ford, *Morality, Identity and Narrative*, which reads him in the context of the theories of Paul Ricoeur and Alasdair MacIntyre.

19. Michael Cathcart, interview with Richard Ford, Australian Broadcasting Corporation, July 21, 2012. Ford also connects his own work to Emerson's in the video interview "Richard Ford on *Lay of the Land* Part 2," YouTube, 2 March 2011, http://www.youtube.com/watch?v=8xWgp9TjxDA. In *Independence Day*, Ford's most explicitly Emersonian novel, Frank gives his son Paul copies of Emerson's "Self-Reliance" and Carl Becker's *Declaration of Independence* as "key texts" for "transmitting to him important info" and notes that "these volumes by the way aren't a bit grinding, stuffy or boring, the way they seemed in school, but are brimming with useful, insightful lessons applicable directly or metaphorically to the ropy dilemmas of life" (8). For discussions of Carl Becker as a pragmatist historian, see Strout, *The Pragmatic Revolt*; and Kloppenberg, "Pragmatism and the Practice of History."

20. For useful discussions of Emerson's relationship to the American pragmatist tradition, see Dolan, *Emerson's Liberalism*; and West, *The American Evasion.*

21. See Poirier, *The Renewal of Literature* and *Poetry and Pragmatism*; Levin, *The Poetics of Transition*; Richardson, *A Natural History of Pragmatism.* Lisi Schoenbach's recent book, *Pragmatic Modernism*, although not Emersonian, also connects pragmatism strongly to literary modernism.

22. Williams James notes in *Pragmatism* (Lecture 6): "Truth is *made*, just as health, wealth and strength are made, in the course of experience" (*Writings 1902–1910*, 581).

23. Richard Ford himself makes this point, in a less direct way, in his introduction

to the first volume of *The Granta Book of the American Short Story*, where, having spent some time juggling the competing claims of experimentalism and tradition, he suggests that the energies of the postmodern short story can be, and probably already have been, absorbed into realism. Remembering his thoughts on the emergence of writers such as Donald Barthelme, John Barth, and William H. Gass in the 1960s and 1970s, he notes:

> To me, the new work all around was thrilling, but so was the old, and as a reader I didn't see a need to choose, though my tendencies as a writer were toward the traditional. There were extremes of form—I understood that. But if in stories yet to be written, these extremes could be made by writers to accommodate one another—contrary formal features joined, language's "poetic qualities" recertified for wider use—then change, even *refinement* would occur. And probably, I thought, they would occur in the context of traditional convictions proving resilient. That, I thought would be the short story's future. (x–xi)

Critic Robert Rebein also makes essentially the same point in *Hicks, Tribes and Dirty Realists* when he suggests that "contemporary realist writers have *absorbed* postmodernism's most lasting contributions and gone on to forge a new realism that is more or less traditional in its handling of character, reportorial in its depiction of milieu and time, but is at the same time self-conscious about language and the limits of mimesis" (20). This idea—that realism can and has absorbed certain elements from modernism and postmodernism while still remaining identifiably realist—is of central importance, I would suggest, to any attempt to adequately describe and account for contemporary realist fiction. My argument in this book usefully extends Rebein's, I hope, by exploring the possibility that the American pragmatist tradition may offer the key to understanding the form and implications of such borrowings.

24. Ford, "The Three Kings," 285.

25. Ford, *The Sportswriter*, 101. Hereafter cited in the text as *S*.

26. I am thinking, for example, of Lionel Trilling's well-known assertion at the end of the preface to *The Liberal Imagination* that "the job of criticism would seem to be . . . to recall liberalism to its first essential imagination of variousness and possibility, which implies the awareness of complexity and difficulty."

27. Franzen, *How to Be Alone*, 67.

28. Franzen's general lack of sympathy with literary experimentation is indeed made abundantly clear in his essay on William Gaddis, "Mr. Difficult," first published in the *New Yorker* in September 2002 and then republished in *How to Be Alone*. He notes that "the essence of postmodernism is an adolescent celebration of consciousness, an adolescent fear of getting taken in, an adolescent conviction that all systems are phony" (268).

29. Franzen, *How to Be Alone*, 91–92.

30. Poirier, *The Renewal of Literature*, 192–93. Rorty's relationship to European poststructuralism and the work of Derrida in particular is certainly complicated, and

critics have spent a good deal of time and energy attempting to properly describe and assess it. What I am pointing to here is Rorty's consistent suggestion that American pragmatism should be seen as part of an historicist and antifoundationalist tradition that begins with Hegel and runs through Nietzsche, Heidegger, and Wittgenstein before reaching Derrida, whom he saw as its most original and interesting contemporary representative. This is not to say that Rorty agreed with everything Derrida wrote (he didn't) or to downplay his dislike of the literary deconstruction he saw practiced by many of Derrida's American followers. For Rorty's own account of his relationship with Derrida and deconstruction, see "Deconstruction and Circumvention." For a broader discussion of the same issues, see Mouffe, *Deconstruction and Pragmatism.* Thomas McCarthy in "Private Irony" and "Ironist Theory" offers a useful correction to Rorty's efforts to link American pragmatism to the Nietzsche, Heidegger, Derrida line.

31. Posnock, *Philip Roth's Rude Truth*, 9. Richard Rorty similarly admits that his version of Dewey leaves out certain important aspects of Dewey's original thought; see "Dewey between Hegel and Darwin."

32. Emerson, *The Collected Works*, 3:35.

33. James, *Writings 1902–1910*, 588.

34. Dewey, *Experience and Nature*, 421.

35. James, *Writings 1902–1910*, 925.

36. My argument here is similar in spirit but crucially different in the details from Alan Wilde's argument in *Middle Grounds.* Wilde suggests that critics of contemporary fiction should focus their attention on the middle ground between "the oppositional extremes of realism on one hand and world denying reflexivity on the other" (4). He is surely right to insist that the idea that literary representation is more or less impossible is as unhelpful (for the contemporary writer and the contemporary critic) as the idea that it is more or less unproblematic. He is wrong, though, I think, to conclude from this that traditional realism is no longer "a major option for most serious writers" (22). Whereas I place Richard Ford squarely in this middle ground, Wilde's main example of what *he* means by it is the work of Donald Barthelme.

37. Ford, *Independence Day*, 94. Hereafter cited in the text as *ID.*

38. James, *Writings 1902–1910*, 509.

39. Ford, *The Lay of the Land*, 475. Hereafter cited in the text as *LL.*

40. Ford, *Canada*, 398. Hereafter cited in the text as *C.*

41. Emerson, *The Collected Works*, 3:39.

42. Ibid., 6:26–27.

43. "The doings and sufferings that form experience are, in the degree in which experience is intelligent or charged with meanings, a union of the precarious, novel, irregular with the settled, assured and uniform—a union which also defines the artistic and the esthetic. For wherever there is art the contingent and ongoing no longer work at cross-purposes with the formal and recurrent but commingle in harmony" (Dewey, *Experience and Nature*, 358–59).

1. The Lie of Literature and the Work of Mourning

1. It is for this reason that I do not discuss *A Piece of My Heart* and *The Ultimate Good Luck* at any length in this book. Both novels seem to me to be apprentice works that are less successful and also distinctly different in tone and theme from the later novels and short stories. My knowledge of Ford's history of reading Emerson comes from a personal email correspondence.

2. Shoup, "Interview with Richard Ford."

3. *Night Wing*, Frank tells us, was the story of

> a bemused young southerner who joins the Navy but gets discharged with a mysterious disease, goes to New Orleans and loses himself into a hazy world of sex and drugs and rumored gun-running and a futile attempt to reconcile a vertiginous present with the guilty memories of not dying alongside his Navy comrades, all of which is climaxed in a violent tryst with a Methodist minister's wife who seduces him in an abandoned slave-quarters, though other times too, after which his life is shattered and he disappears permanently into the Texas oil fields. It was all told in a series of flashbacks. (*S*, 36)

4. Frank sees the potential for suggestive mystery in religion and art, but he also sees it in his parents' rather more mundane decision not to explain certain "adult" facts about their lives to him when he was young: "They were my parents—higher in terms absolute and unknowable. I didn't know how they financed their cars. When they made love or how they liked it. Who they had their insurance with. What their doctor told them privately (though they must've both heard bad news eventually). They simply loved me, and I them. The rest, they didn't feel the need to blab about. That there should always be something important I wouldn't know, but could wonder at, wander near, yet never be certain about was, as far as I'm concerned, their greatest gift and lesson" (*S*, 205).

5. Shoup, "Interview with Richard Ford."

6. In the same interview with Barbara Shoup, Ford describes Lish as "a big influence in my life in a kind of bad way. He was a sort of Mephistophelian character in my life for about ten years."

7. Guagliardo, *Conversations*, 172.

8. Ibid., 12.

9. "There was really just too much of everything in *Absalom, Absalom!* Life, in words, geysering and eddying over each other, so that just being sure what was what and who was who became challenge enough to make you beg off choosing among what things might formally *mean*—a valuable enough lesson, certainly for anyone who wants to learn about anything, ever" (Ford, "The Three Kings," 282).

10. Ibid., 284–85.

11. Guagliardo, *Conversations*, 12.

12. Ibid., 12, 189.

13. Ibid., 158.

14. Ford, "My Mother, in Memory," 56.

15. Guagliardo, *Conversations*, 28.

16. Freud, *The Standard Edition*, 14:255. To be clear, my use of Freud and Melanie Klein here and later in chapter 4 is instrumental and pragmatic. I am using psychoanalytic theory as a tool to better demonstrate and explain what is going on in Richard Ford's fiction, to unpack certain episodes, characters, and contexts that might otherwise remain elusive. I am not asking readers to accept Freud's theories in toto, in other words, but rather to see some of the language and ideas of psychoanalysis as useful and relevant in particular circumstances. Although it is nearly a hundred years old now, Freud's famous essay remains, I would argue, the unavoidable starting point for any serious discussion of the psychology of mourning.

17. The very first word of *Rock Springs* is "Edna," the name of Ford's mother, and the very last words at the end of "Communist" are "my mother and I never talked in that way again, and I have not heard her voice now in a long, long time" (Ford, *Rock Springs*, 1, 235; hereafter cited in the text as *RS*).

18. According to an interview, Ford wrote the story in February 1981 (Guagliardo, *Conversations*, 108). The essay "My Mother, in Memory" (although vague on specific dates) makes clear that Ford was painfully aware of her impending death some time before that: "I read my mother's death in almost all of her life during those days. I looked for illness. Listened to her complaints too carefully. Planned her death obscurely, along with my own abhorrence of it—treated myself to it early so that when the time came I would not, myself, go down completely" (55).

19. Guagliardo, *Conversations*, 38.

20. Klein, *Love, Guilt and Reparation*, 355.

21. Sacks, *The English Elegy*, 232.

22. A brief but interesting passage in "The Three Kings" essay opens up the intriguing possibility that this hard-boiled Hemingwayesque style may itself be a way of invoking, perhaps even keeping alive, the mother. Ford remembers that he first became aware of Hemingway when he was sixteen, because his mother admired Hemingway's "rough yet sensitive" appearance and his "resolution and certainty about first principles." He concludes with the observations that his mother "was the first person I knew who was truly Hemingwayesque. And that included Ernest Hemingway himself" (279–80).

23. One of the peculiarities of *Wildlife* (1990) and possibly one reason why it is Ford's least successful novel is that it seems to combine the style and milieu of *Rock Springs* with the consolatory conclusions of *The Sportswriter*.

24. Sacks, *The English Elegy*, 313. Jahan Ramazani, in *Poetry of Mourning*, argues that the modern poetic elegy is in general antagonistic toward inherited elegiac conventions.

25. The connection between the suburbs and pastoralism in *The Sportswriter* is made most explicit in the following passage from the beginning of chapter 12:

> It is the bottom of the day, the deep well of shadows and springy half-light when late afternoon becomes early evening and we all want to sit down in a leather chair by an open window, have a drink near someone we love or like, read the sports and possibly doze for a while, then wake before the day is gone all the way, walk our cool yards and hear the birds chirp in the trees their sweet eventide songs. It is for such dewy interludes that the suburbs were built. And entered cautiously, they can serve us well no matter what our stations in life, no matter we have the aforementioned liberty or don't. At times I can long so for that simple measure of day and place . . . that an unreasonable tear nearly comes to my eye. It's a pastoral kind of longing, of course, but we can all have it. (312)

26. Ford has been very clear about his intention in the Bascombe trilogy to represent the suburbs in a newly positive way. In a 2007 *California Literary Review* interview with David Cross on *The Lay of the Land*, Ford says of the suburbs:

> They're around us all the time, even if you live in the city. It's part of our environment. And just to always have, as our attitude, this is crap, this is crap, this is crap, this is horrible, this is an eyesore, I hate this. Have it always be your mantra didn't seem so healthy. And it would be, at least—as a provisional way, not as a final judgment about the suburbs, but as a provisional way—see if I couldn't generate a vocabulary of affirmation for what was traditionally and conventionally thought of as not affirmable. And, you know, I could have done the traditional thing, written that there's just a lot of rubbish here. But actually when I wrote it, I thought this is good. I liked it. It was a literary strategy that became sort of a life strategy. That's generally how things work with me. I write these things out in a book. I try these things out by writing them. You know, Cheever and Yates and Roth, lots of people have taken the piss out of the suburbs, so I just thought, well, I'm going to do something else.

The originality of this approach is perhaps underlined by the hostile misreading of the Bascombe novels in Catherine Jurca's *White Diaspora*, 169–71. Jurca is clearly much more comfortable with the mainstream antisuburban tradition, which she carefully traces, than with Ford's revisionism. She find's Frank's optimism "insufferable" and "condescending" and ends by linking his attitude to the recent spread of gated communities.

27. Sacks, *The English Elegy*, 315.

28. Brown, *The Emerson Museum*, 46.

29. For a detailed and convincing consideration of Ellison's relationship to the broader pragmatic tradition, see Posnock, *Color and Culture.*

30. Ellison, *Invisible Man*, 464.

31. For a detailed discussion of Ellison's relationship to the American canon, see Nadel, "The Integrated Literary Tradition."

32. Ford, "The Three Kings," 282.

33. Marx, *The Machine in the Garden.*

34. "Nothing is secure but life, transition, the energizing spirit. No love can be bound by oath or covenant to secure it against a higher love. No truth so sublime but it may be trivial tomorrow in the light of new thoughts. People wish to be settled: only in so far as they are unsettled, is there any hope for them" (Emerson, *The Collected Works*, 2:189). The previous quotation is from the same volume and page.

35. Ibid., 3:29.

2. *Independence Day* and the Limits of Pragmatism

1. Emerson, *The Collected Works*, 3:46.

2. Rorty refers approvingly (and frequently) to Nietzsche's description of truth as a "mobile army of metaphors" and in "The Contingency of Language" notes that intellectual and moral progress is "a history of increasingly useful metaphors rather than of increasing understanding of how things really are" (*Contingency*, 9).

3. For the Emersonian, as "The Divinity School Address" famously makes clear, "it is not instruction, but provocation, that I can receive from another soul" (Emerson, *The Collected Works*, 1:80).

4. Rorty, *Philosophy*, 82.

5. Michel de Certeau makes a very similar point about the differences between elevated and ground-level perspectives in *The Practice of Everyday Life*, 91–93. Philosophically speaking, the contrast is between totalization or commensurability, on the one hand, and difference or incommensurability, on the other. When taken to an extreme, an emphasis on incommensurability may become relativistic and quite possibly incoherent (as Hilary Putnam has interestingly argued; see *Reason, Truth and History*, 113–19). However, in this section of *Independence Day*, Frank's suggestion works as a practical and cheerful corrective to Joe's failed idealism.

6. Baudrillard, *America*; Jameson, *Postmodernism.*

7. My reading of this section of the novel raises the complex question of the relationship between pragmatism and postmodernism. I believe Ford's version of pragmatism, in *Independence Day* and elsewhere, ultimately sets itself *against* a hedonic postmodernism characterized by pastiche and eclecticism. This issue is discussed much more fully in the next two chapters, but to anticipate my own argument a little, we might say that for Ford, true self-reliance finally involves a complex double movement whereby the past is both recognized and moved away from, rather than the playful or therapeutic reshufflings of the past characteristic of the more celebratory forms of postmodernism.

8. Although the Markhams do eventually instruct Frank to make an offer on a house, they delay too long, and the house is sold to someone else.

9. Bloom, *The Anxiety of Influence.*

10. Wallace Stevens has been connected to the pragmatist tradition by Richard Poirier in *The Renewal of Literature* and also by Jonathan Levin in *The Poetics of Transition* and Joan Richardson in *A Natural History of Pragmatism.*

11. Frank insists on Ann's status as a crude metaphysician: "This is the perpetual theme of her life: the search for truth and truth's defeat by the forces of contingency, most frequently represented by yours truly" (*ID*, 253).

12. Edmundson, *Towards Reading Freud*, 145.

13. Poirier, *The Renewal of Literature*, 178.

14. Edmundson, *Towards Reading Freud*, 144.

15. This kind of criticism goes back as far as Hawthorne and Melville. Sidney Hook attempted to refute it in 1974 in *Pragmatism and the Tragic Sense of Life*, but it persists and can be seen more recently (albeit in quite different forms) in the work of Raymond Boisvert, Terry Eagleton (in *Sweet Violence*), and Stanley Cavell. Cavell, for example, in his attempt to reclaim Emerson for Continental philosophy, claims that from an "Emersonian" perspective "the Deweyan is apt to seem an enlightened child, toying with the means of destruction, stinting the means of instruction" (*Conditions Handsome and Unhandsome*, 16). For Cavell, philosophy, or thinking, begins with a profound and inescapable sense of loss, which pragmatism as a practical problem-solving approach is either unaware of or uninterested in.

16. Rorty, *Contingency*, 40.

17. Emerson, *The Collected Works*, 6:11.

18. This broadly dialectical pattern—hope, followed by disillusionment, followed by another kind of hope—defines the narrative arc of all three novels in the Bascombe trilogy. Each one works up to a dramatic climax (on the lawn of the Arcenault house in *The Sportswriter*, in the batting cage at Cooperstown in *Independence Day*, and at the Manasquan Bar in *The Lay of the Land*) in which Frank's hopeful efforts to escape the loss of Ralph and all that loss symbolizes fail and after which he is required to begin again—not to abandon optimism and hope entirely but to in some way reimagine them.

19. The tension between individualism and social cohesion has been a central concern of American thinkers (liberal thinkers especially) since Tocqueville. Quentin Anderson's *The Imperial Self* is still perhaps the best-known communitarian critique of the individualist tradition. For a recent, nonliterary reiteration of these long-running concerns, see Putnam, *Bowling Alone.*

20. The intellectual origins of this dilemma are glimpsed in *Independence Day* when before the accident Frank thinks about introducing his son to Emerson's "Self-Reliance": "In particular I might try out the astute 'Discontent is the want of self-reliance; it is infirmity of will.' Or else something on the order of accepting the place providence has found for you, the society of your contemporaries, the connection of events. Each seems to me immensely serviceable if, however, they aren't contradictory" (*ID*, 264).

21. Rorty, *Contingency*, 83.

22. Ibid., 89.

23. Ibid., 92.

24. In an interview with Sophie Majeski shortly after the publication of *Independence Day*, he noted:

> But when I started writing about Frank at the beginning of the book, I kept thinking to myself, what the hell is at issue here? . . . [S]o I thought to myself, well, he has an equilibrium in his life which he has paid the price of isolation to maintain. . . . [W]hat price have you paid to attain equilibrium? And what I figured out was that the price Frank had paid—and it was a high price—was that he was isolated and had achieved independence only in a conditional sense. And what was at issue in his life was how in the process of maintaining that equilibrium he could ever touch somebody. How could he run the risk of complicating his life by engaging people he cared about? So that is what the book is about.

25. Rorty, *Contingency*, 92.

26. Rorty suggests that even in an ideal liberal society the public-private distinction would still operate: "I cannot . . . claim that there could or ought to be a culture whose public rhetoric is *ironist.* I cannot imagine a culture which socialized its youth in such a way as to make them continually dubious about their own process of socialization. Irony seems inherently a private matter" (*Contingency*, 87).

27. In a crucial moment toward the end of *The Sportswriter*, after Walter Luckett's suicide, Frank symbolically leaves home, abandoning Walter's flat and jumping on a train to New York, where new opportunities present themselves.

28. For references to existentialism, see, for example, *The Lay of the Land*, 210, 326.

3. "Spoiled People"

1. Frederic Jameson, "Afterword: A Note on Literary Realism," in Beaumont, *A Concise Companion*, 279–89.

2. Ford, *A Multitude of Sins*, 20. Hereafter cited in the text as *MS*.

3. Ford, *Women with Men*, 171. Hereafter cited in the text as *WM*.

4. In the provocative and hyperbolic *Still the New World*, Fisher argues that America and its literature is defined by a process of creative destruction in which each generation starts afresh and in which immigration (or "removal") is thus "a life form and not simply a onetime act" (272). In *Philip Roth's Rude Truth*, Posnock places Philip Roth within a literary and intellectual tradition of transgressive immaturity that is at the same time Emersonian, pragmatic, and modernist. He emphasizes, above all, Roth's refusal to conform to any predetermined role or expectation, his desire to always remain on the move. Fiedler notes in the introduction to *Love and Death in the American Novel* that ever since Rip Van Winkle "the typical male protagonist of our fiction has been a man on the run, harried into the forest and out to sea, down the river or into combat—anywhere to avoid 'civilisation,' which is to say the confrontation of

a man and a woman which leads to the fall, to sex, marriage, and responsibility" (xx).

5. Fiedler suggests in typically robust fashion that the three main options available to a male American protagonist fleeing the confines of domesticity are impotence, innocent homosexuality, and unconsummated incest (ibid., 343). Fisher and Posnock emphasize in contrast the importance of pragmatic or aesthetic self-creation, but neither set of possibilities, the darkly Freudian or the more hopefully pragmatic, fully captures Matthews's position.

6. For a discussion of the historical transition from modernist alienation to postmodernist fragmentation, see Jameson, *Postmodernism*, 1–16.

7. The classic articulations of this position are Roland Barthes's 1967 essay "The Death of the Author," and Jacques Derrida's 1966 lecture "Structure, Sign and Play." In the latter work, Derrida uses "center" as a synecdoche for structure more generally and identifies a recent "rupture" or "event" that we may plausibly identify as the beginnings of postmodernism and that he describes as the moment when "language invaded the universal problematic, the moment when, in the absence of a center or origin, everything became discourse" (280).

8. Fiedler had little time for Emerson (who is barely mentioned in *Love and Death in the American Novel*), but Emerson is central to both Fisher and Posnock. The central importance of Emerson to the development of America's literary *and* philosophical traditions has been convincingly argued for by a number of recent critics, most notably Richard Poirier. See, for example, Poirier's *Poetry and Pragmatism* and Cornel West's *The American Evasion of Philosophy*.

9. The connections between American pragmatism and Continental philosophy are most energetically and thoroughly examined in the work of Richard Rorty. See note 30 in the introduction above.

10. Putnam, *Realism with a Human Face*, 118. The differences I am pointing to here are essentially ones of degree and emphasis. Whereas postmodern thinkers emphasize the deconstructive or negative aspect of a post-Kantian critique of reason, classical (i.e., non-Rortyan) pragmatist thinkers attempt to strike a balance between the negative and the positive, deconstruction and reconstruction. I am using "relativism" in this chapter as a simplifying but, I think, still legitimate shorthand for the postmodernist position. Supporters of Foucault and Derrida are, of course, unlikely to agree with my position, but the arguments on both sides are too lengthy and too abstruse to fully rehearse here. Thomas McCarthy's *Ideals and Illusions* gives a good overall account of the pragmatist/Habermasian position; for an example of opposing views, see Gutting, *Michel Foucault's Archaeology*, 272–87.

11. "Standing on the bare ground—my head bathed by the blithe air and uplifted into infinite space—all mean egotism vanishes. I become a transparent eyeball; I am nothing; I see all; the currents of the Universal Being circulate through me; I am part or parcel of God. The name of the nearest friend sounds then foreign and accidental: to be brothers, to be acquaintances, master or servant is then a trifle and a disturbance" (Emerson, *The Collected Works*, 1:10).

12. Although in his discussion of "democratic social space" Fisher does not acknowledge any debt to Lefebvre, the connections are clear enough. See Lefebvre, *The Production of Space.*

13. Fisher, *Still the New World*, 49.

14. The notion of the city as a place of irrationality, disorder, and postmodern "play" has been articulated most notably by Certeau in *The Practice of Everyday Life.*

15. The same terminology is used by Lefebvre, although with entirely opposite political implications.

16. For a more detailed account of this argument, see Putnam, *Reason, Truth and History*, 119–24. See also Habermas, *The Philosophical Discourse*, and, for a discussion of how Putnam's ideas may relate to literary criticism, see Nussbaum, "Sophistry about Conventions."

17. Putnam, *Realism with a Human Face*, 120.

18. The most clear and striking example of this paradox within the postmodern canon is the hallucinatory antirealism of Jean Baudrillard, where the hyperreal frequently takes on the qualities of absolute truth. In *Fatal Strategies*, for example, Baudrillard notes: "Just as the model is more real than the real . . . the amazing aspect of fashion is that it is more beautiful than the beautiful. . . . It exceeds the aesthetic form in the ecstatic form of unconditional metamorphosis" (Poster, *Jean Baudrillard*, 186).

19. Freud's classic essay "On Narcissism: An Introduction" (*The Standard Edition*, 14:67–102) has surprisingly little to say about the specific ways in which narcissistic disorders develop. Melanie Klein and her followers, however, offer a more detailed account. Paula Heiman notes, for example: "In the narcissistic condition the external object is hated and rejected, so that one loves the internal object which is fused with the self and experiences pleasure from it. The external object and its inner representation (gained through introjection) are thus sharply divided. However, the technique of splitting the object into two derives from and presupposes the fundamental premise that somewhere the two are only one" (Klein et al., *Developments*, 153–54).

20. Narcissism is an accusation that has been leveled at Americans before, of course; see, most notably, Anderson, *The Imperial Self*; Lasch, *The Culture of Narcissism.* Both Anderson and Lasch see narcissism as an unfortunate side effect of American individualism and, in particular, of American culture's long-standing disdain for fathers (both literal and symbolic). Matthews's relationship with his actual father (who runs a furniture business in Pittsburgh) remains quite vague in "Occidentals," but the story begins with him being painfully disillusioned by his French editor, François Blumberg, a man he has previously imagined in distinctly and sentimentally paternal terms: "From their correspondence, Matthews had always pictured François Blumberg as an old man, a kindly keeper of an ancient flame, overseer of a rich and storied culture that only a few were permitted to share" (*WM*, 152).

21. This idea of the "bad" mother comes from Melanie Klein's object-relations theory. The splitting of the mother (or, more specifically, the breast) into "good" and "bad" versions—the former introjected, the latter projected outward—is typical, according

to Klein, of the paranoid-schizoid position of early infancy, which should be left behind in the process of healthy development. The failure to pass beyond the paranoid-schizoid position is associated with narcissism and a number of other related mental disorders. See Klein's essay "Notes on Some Schizoid Mechanisms," in Mitchell, *The Selected Melanie Klein*, 175–200.

22. In both stories, the inciting "loss" is simultaneously the loss of the mother (or mother substitute) and the loss of a broader sense of epistemological confidence and certainty. It is interesting and relevant in this regard to note how filial affection and knowledge merge in the conclusion of Ford's 1987 autobiographical essay, "My Mother, in Memory," where he notes: "And I have known that moment with her we would all like to know, the moment of saying, 'Yes. This is what it is.' An act of knowing that certifies love. I have known that. I have known any number of such moments with her" (44–57).

23. The aggression toward the "bad mother" is present in the story but is expressed via Joséphine's first husband, Bernard, who writes an autobiographical novel intended to humiliate her.

24. Any definition of what exactly Putnam means by "internal realism" is of necessity partial and broad (since one of the characteristics of internal realism is that it makes no specific universal claims), but the following passage gives a good general sense of what he is aiming at:

> The metaphysical realist insists that a mysterious relationship of "correspondence" is what makes reference and truth possible; the internal realist, by contrast, is willing to think of reference as internal to texts (or theories), *provided* we realise that there are better and worse "texts." "Better" and "worse" may themselves depend on our historical situation and our purposes; there is no notion of a God's-Eye View of Truth here. But the notion of a right (or at least a "better") answer to a question is subject to two constraints: (1) *Rightness is not subjective* . . . (2) *Rightness goes beyond justification*. (*Realism with a Human Face*, 114)

Putnam wishes to argue (here and elsewhere) that there *are* objective criteria for making ethical and philosophical judgments, of "better" and "worse," but that those criteria change over time and according to circumstances and therefore cannot be specified in advance: "The assertability conditions for an arbitrary sentence are not surveyable" (ibid., 115).

25. The dating of the story is suggestive, since the postmodern era is often seen as beginning with the oil crisis of 1973.

26. "We have discovered, especially clearly in people whose libidinal development has suffered some disturbance, such as perverts and homosexuals, that in their later choice of love objects they have taken as a model not their mother but their own selves. They are plainly seeking *themselves* as a love-object, and are exhibiting a type of object-choice which must be termed 'narcissistic'" (Freud, *The Standard Edition*, 14:88).

27. For an example of such a critique, see Fredric Jameson's reading of dirty realism in *Seeds of Time*, 144–59.

28. Madame de Grenelle is of "mixed race" (Matthews speculates that she is Berber) and shares her house with another woman.

29. Putnam, *Reason, Truth and History*, 114.

30. Ibid., 117.

31. Here D. W. Winnicott's famous remark that "it is a joy to be hidden but a disaster not to be found" may be of relevance. Winnicott's argument is that the self is essentially secret (i.e., incommensurable), yet it is also and equally importantly defined by the continual need to communicate. For a useful discussion of this aspect of Winnicott's ideas, see Phillips, *Winnicott*, 138–52.

4. "What Was That Thing She Was?"

1. The idea of violent death as an ontological bottom line in comparison with which most other things appear thin or secondary is embodied, for example, in the contrapuntal structure of Hemingway's *In Our Time*. It also occurs frequently in existentialist writing as a guarantor of the absurdity of human existence, Camus's *The Fall* being a particularly relevant example. Earlier critics of Ford have often emphasized his connection to existentialist ideas and themes. In his introduction to *Perspectives on Richard Ford*, for example, Huey Guagliardo notes that while the essays in the collection "employ a variety of critical perspectives, they all place Ford's texts within the framework of the literature of alienation" (xii). My argument here is that, in *Multitude of Sins* at least, his work includes these concerns but also goes beyond them.

2. Nochlin, *The Body in Pieces*, 55.

3. Foster, "Obscene, Abject, Traumatic." In literary theory this abject strain of postmodernism can be linked to the emergence of trauma as an important critical category, a development that occurred first in the mid-1990s with works by Cathy Caruth, Dominick LaCapra, and Mark Seltzer and that then was given increased impetus by the terrorist attacks of September 2001.

4. Ibid., 123.

5. Howard enrages Frances by describing the canyon as "big, but . . . empty" (*MS*, 272). He describes it to himself in even more damning terms as "sort of useless. A negative" (*MS*, 271).

6. The fact that the fragmented body in both "Quality Time" and "Abyss" is a female body suggests the limited and conventional nature of Ford's understanding of gender in this collection. In both stories there is an implicit association of femininity with the body and nature and masculinity with culture and the mind. This means that the alternatives thrown up by postmodern culture—hyperreality versus disintegration—are almost always gendered, the former male and the latter female. Although I have been arguing that ultimately Ford sees both sides of the duality as linked and equally unappealing, the division of symbolic labor is hardly equal.

7. The idea that postmodernism has no "outside" is a development of the idea, strongly associated with French poststructuralism (although clearly prefigured in the work of Nietzsche and Wittgenstein), that the world is only available to us via

language. The tendency to interpret this idea in sociological terms as indicating the necessary limits of any kind of oppositional activity is usually linked directly or indirectly to the ideas of Michel Foucault and has been most successfully promulgated within the Anglo-American academy by the hugely influential work of Judith Butler.

8. While adultery appears in the nineteenth-century novel as the definitive act of transgression against the structures and conventions of bourgeois society—the act that lays bare the various tensions and contradictions inherent in a particular, quite specific social order—in the postmodern context of *A Multitude of Sins*, adultery has become, for the most part, a pastiche, a set of empty gestures whose transgressive power has long since dispersed. Ford's lovers play out familiar, inherited roles that have been drained of any ethical or emotional meaning. In "Quality Time" Wales and Jena, for example, worry that a knock on the hotel door means the arrival of a jealous husband when we have already been told that Jena's husband is quite happy for her to have affairs. In "Dominion" the female partner hires an actor to play the part of her enraged husband in order to make the end of her affair feel more believable.

9. In "Puppy" Sallie's affair with her husband's law partner is linked to death indirectly via the assumed demise of the puppy of the title and more directly by Sallie's recurrent "war dreams," "[t]echnicolor nightmares without plots or coherent scenarios" that feature "images of dismembered bodies flying around" (*MS*, 84). Similarly, in "Under the Radar" Marjorie's adultery is connected symbolically to the crippled raccoon that she urges her husband to get out of their car to help and also, less symbolically, to her husband's probable death or injury in the story's final lines, when Marjorie appears set to run him down.

10. "Fucking Crystal [Tom's girlfriend]," we are told, was in part "a result of pure exhilaration about his new life, something he needed to celebrate on his own and in his own way—a 'universe' feeling he called it, wherein acts took place outside the boundaries of convention, obligation, the past and even good sense (just as events occurred in the universe)" (*MS*, 184–85).

11. Rorty's summary of Dewey's position is in Rorty, *Consequences*, 207; Foucault, *The Archaeology of Knowledge*, 229.

12. Habermas discusses Mead's work in some detail in his *Theory of Communicative Action*, vol. 2. He suggests that Mead's ideas, like his own, are based on the utopian ideal of a "communication community" in which social norms can be democratically and rationally agreed upon and modified. Habermas believes that such an ideal is implicit in all linguistic and symbolic interactions, and this forms the basis of his defense of reason as a liberating rather than an oppressive force. For a useful discussion of the relationship between Mead and Habermas, see Dews, "Communicative Paradigms."

13. Mead, *Mind, Self, and Society*, 171.

14. Ibid., 174.

15. Ibid.

16. James, *Writings 1902–1910*, 510.

5. "Everything Good Is on the Highway"

1. Emerson, *The Collected Works*, 2:40.

2. Frank describes the ideal inhabitant of the Permanent Period as "an actualized unchangeable non-becomer, as snugged into life as a planning board member" (*LL*, 75).

3. Knapp, "Richard Ford's Frank Bascombe Trilogy," 518.

4. See, for example, Antonio Monda's interview with Ford in *Do You Believe?*

5. Richard Poirier asks, for example, "How do we experience a 'transition'?" and answers: "I suggest, tentatively, that it is like catching a glimpse of a thing before it is possible to recognize or name it, the moment before it can be classified by language and thus become composed or reposed in a human corpus or text" (*The Renewal of Literature*, 47).

6. Emerson, *The Collected Works*, 4:32.

7. Levin, *The Poetics of Transition*, 3.

8. For the classic narratological account of the relationship between scene and summary, see Genette, *Narrative Discourse*, 86–112.

9. It is also present in the more minor form of Frank's remembering or talking about his dead son, Ralph, in the scene with Tom Benivalle, the scene at the De Tocqueville Academy with Anne, and the scene at the Johnny Appleseed Bar.

10. Kermode, *The Sense of an Ending.* Ford has mentioned Kermode's book approvingly in several interviews, for example, Bush and Arroyo, "The Measure and Style."

11. "It is for want of self-culture that the superstition of Travelling, whose idols are Italy, England, Egypt, retains its fascination for all educated Americans. They who made England, Italy, or Greece venerable in the imagination, did so by sticking fast where they were, like an axis of the earth. In manly hours, we feel that duty is our place" (Emerson, *The Collected Works*, 2:46).

12. Ibid., 2:28.

13. James, *Writings 1902–1910*, 748–50.

14. Ibid., 751.

15. Emerson, *The Collected Works*, 2:29.

16. Dewey, *Experience and Nature*, 410.

17. Emerson, *The Collected Works*, 3:39.

18. Ibid., 3:36.

Conclusion. *Canada* and the Hazards of Normality

1. Emerson, *The Collected Works*, 3:35.

2. Ibid.

3. Dewey, *Experience and Nature*, 16.

BIBLIOGRAPHY

Anderson, Quentin. *The Imperial Self.* New York: Knopf, 1971.

Armengol, Josep M. *Richard Ford and the Fiction of Masculinities.* New York: Peter Lang, 2010.

Barthes, Roland. "The Death of the Author." In *Image, Music, Text*, 142–48. London: Fontana, 1977.

———. *The Rustle of Language.* Translated by Richard Howard. Oxford: Basil Blackwell, 1986.

Baudrillard, Jean. *America.* London: Verso, 1988.

Beaumont, Matthew, ed. *A Concise Companion to Realism.* Oxford: Blackwell, 2010.

Belsey, Catherine. *Critical Practice.* London: Routledge, 1980.

Bloom, Harold. *The Anxiety of Influence: A Theory of Poetry.* New York: Oxford University Press, 1973.

Bone, Martyn. *The Postsouthern Sense of Place in Contemporary Fiction.* Baton Rouge: Louisiana State University Press, 2005.

Bové, Paul A. Review of *Literature against Itself: Literary Ideas in Modern Society*, by Gerald Graff. *Criticism* 22, no. 1 (Winter 1980): 77–81.

Brown, Lee Rust. *The Emerson Museum: Practical Romanticism and the Pursuit of the Whole.* Cambridge, MA: Harvard University Press, 1997.

Bush, Harold K., and Fred Arroyo. "The Measure and Style of Acceptance: A Conversation with Richard Ford." *Michigan Quarterly Review* 47, no. 4 (Fall 2008), http://hdl.handle.net/2027/spo.act2080.0047.401.

Butler, Judith. *Gender Trouble: Feminism and the Subversion of Identity.* London: Routledge, 2006.

Caruth, Cathy. *Unclaimed Experience: Trauma, Narrative, and History.* Baltimore, MD: Johns Hopkins University Press, 1996.

Cathcart, Michael. Interview with Richard Ford. Australian Broadcasting Corporation, July 21, 2012.

Cavell, Stanley. *Conditions Handsome and Unhandsome: The Constitution of Emersonian Perfectionism.* Chicago: University of Chicago Press, 1990.

Certeau, Michel de. *The Practice of Everyday Life.* Berkeley: University of California Press, 1984.

Chernecky, William G. "'Nostalgia Ain't What It Used to Be': Isolation and Alienation in the Frank Bascombe Novels." In *Perspectives on Richard Ford*, edited by Huey Guagliardo, 157–76. Jackson: University Press of Mississippi, 2000.

Cleary, Joe. "Realism after Modernism and the Literary World System." *Modern Language Quarterly* 73, no. 3 (September 2011): 255–68.

Cohen, Samuel. *After the End of History: American Fiction in the 1990s.* Iowa City: University of Iowa Press, 2009.

Cronan, Todd. Review of *The Affect Theory Reader. Radical Philosophy* 172 (March/April 2012): 51–53.

Cross, David. "An Interview with Novelist Richard Ford." *California Literary Review*, March 30, 2007, http://calitreview.com/54.

Derrida, Jacques. "Structure, Sign and Play in the Discourse of the Human Sciences." In *Writing and Difference*, 278–93. Chicago: University of Chicago Press, 1978.

Dewey, John. *Experience and Nature.* Chicago: Open Court, 1925.

———. *The Later Works 1925–1953,* vol. 14, edited by Jo Ann Boydston. Carbondale: Southern Illinois University Press, 2008.

Dewey, Joseph. *Novels from Reagan's America: A New Realism.* Tallahassee: University Press of Florida, 1999.

Dews, Peter. "Communicative Paradigms and the Question of Subjectivity: Habermas, Mead, and Lacan." In *Habermas: A Critical Reader*, edited by Peter Dews, 87–117. Oxford: Blackwell, 1999.

Dolan, Neal. *Emerson's Liberalism.* Madison: University of Wisconsin Press, 2009.

Duffy, Brian. *Morality, Identity and Narrative in the Fiction of Richard Ford.* Amsterdam: Rodopi, 2008.

Eagleton, Terry. *Sweet Violence: The Idea of the Tragic.* Oxford: Blackwell, 2003.

Edmundson, Mark. *Towards Reading Freud: Self-Creation in Milton, Wordsworth, Emerson and Sigmund Freud.* Chicago: University of Chicago Press, 1990.

Eliot, T. S. "*Ulysses*, Order and Myth." In *Selected Prose of T. S. Eliot*, edited by Frank Kermode, 175–78. London: Faber and Faber, 1975.

Ellison, Ralph. *Invisible Man.* London: Penguin, 1965.

Emerson, Ralph Waldo. *The Collected Works of Ralph Waldo Emerson.* 10 vols. to date. Edited by Ronald A. Bosco, Alfred R. Ferguson, Joseph Slater, and Douglas Emory Wilson. Cambridge, MA: Harvard University Press, 1971–.

———. *The Selected Writings of Ralph Waldo Emerson.* New York: Random House, 1992.

Fiedler, Leslie. *Love and Death in the American Novel.* New York: Criterion, 1960.

Fisher, Phillip. *Still the New World: American Literature in a Culture of Creative Destruction.* Cambridge, MA: Harvard University Press, 1999.

Ford, Richard. *Canada.* New York: HarperCollins, 2012.

———. "Good Raymond." *New Yorker*, October 5, 1998, 70–79.

———, ed. *The Granta Book of the American Short Story.* London: Granta, 1992.

———. *Independence Day.* New York: Vintage, 1995.

———. *The Lay of the Land.* New York: Knopf, 2006.

———. *A Multitude of Sins.* New York: Knopf, 2002.

———. "My Mother, in Memory." *Harper's*, August 1987, 44–57.

———. *Rock Springs.* New York: Atlantic, 1987.

———. *The Sportswriter.* New York: Vintage, 1986.

———. "The Three Kings: Faulkner, Hemingway, Fitzgerald" (1983). In *Mississippi Writers: Reflections of Childhood and Youth*, vol. 2, edited by Dorothy Abbott, 275–93. Jackson: University Press of Mississippi, 1986.

———. *Women with Men.* New York: Knopf, 1997.

Foster, Hal. "Obscene, Abject, Traumatic." *October* 78 (Autumn 1996): 106–24.

Foucault, Michel. *The Archaeology of Knowledge.* New York: Harper and Row, 1972.

Franzen, Jonathan. *How to Be Alone.* London: Fourth Estate, 2010.

———. "Mr. Difficult." *New Yorker*, September 30, 2002, 100–111.

Freud, Sigmund. *The Standard Edition of the Complete Psychological Works of Sigmund Freud.* 24 vols. London: Hogarth Press, 1953–74.

Gasché, Rodolphe. "Unscrambling Positions: On Gerald Graff's Critique of Deconstruction." *MLN* 96, no. 5 (December 1981): 1015–34.

Genette, Gerard. *Narrative Discourse: An Essay in Method.* Ithaca, NY: Cornell University Press, 1980.

Graff, Gerald. "Humanism and the Hermeneutics of Power: Reflection on the Hermeneutic Two-Step and Other Dances." *Boundary 2* 12, no. 3 (Spring/Autumn 1984): 495–505.

———. "Is Reason in Trouble?" *Proceedings of the American Philosophical Society* 137, no. 4 (1993): 680–88.

———. *Literature against Itself.* Chicago: Ivan R. Dee, 1995.

———. "Politics, Language, Deconstruction, Lies, and the Reflexive Fallacy: A Rejoinder to W. J. T. Mitchell." *Salmagundi* 47/48 (Winter/Spring 1980): 78–94.

———. "The Pseudo-politics of Interpretation." *Critical Inquiry* 9, no. 3 (March 1983): 597–610.

Guagliardo, Huey, ed. *Conversations with Richard Ford.* Jackson: University Press of Mississippi, 2001.

———. *Perspectives on Richard Ford.* Jackson: University Press of Mississippi, 2000.

Gutting, Gary. *Michel Foucault's Archaeology of Scientific Reason.* Cambridge: Cambridge University Press, 1989.

Habermas, Jürgen. *The Philosophical Discourse of Modernity.* Oxford: Polity, 1987.

———. *Theory of Communicative Action*, vol. 2. Oxford: Polity, 1987.

Haskins, Casey, and David I. Seiple, eds. *Dewey Reconfigured: Essays on Deweyan Pragmatism.* Albany: State University of New York Press, 1999.

Hobson, Fred. "The Sportswriter: Post-Faulkner, Post-Southern?" In *Perspectives on Richard Ford*, edited by Huey Guagliardo, 83–96. Jackson: University Press of Mississippi, 2000.

Hook, Sidney. *Pragmatism and the Tragic Sense of Life.* New York: Basic Books, 1974.

James, William. *Writings 1902–1910.* New York: Library of America, 1987.

Jameson, Fredric. *The Antinomies of Realism*. London: Verso, 2013.

———. *The Political Unconscious: Narrative as Socially Symbolic Act*. Ithaca, NY: Cornell University Press, 1981.

———. *Postmodernism or the Logic of Late Capitalism*. Durham, NC: Duke University Press, 1991.

———. *Seeds of Time*. New York: Columbia University Press, 1994.

Jurca, Catherine. *White Diaspora: The Suburb and the Twentieth Century American Novel*. Princeton, NJ: Princeton University Press, 2001.

Kermode, Frank. *The Sense of an Ending: Studies in the Theory of Fiction*. Cambridge: Cambridge University Press, 1966.

Klein, Melanie. *Love, Guilt and Reparation and Other Works 1921–1954*. London: Vintage, 1998.

Klein, Melanie, Paula Heimann, Susan Isaacs, and Joan Riviere. *Developments in Psycho-analysis* (1952). London: Karnac, 1989.

Kloppenberg, James T. "Pragmatism and the Practice of History: From Turner and Du Bois to Today." In *The Range of Pragmatism and the Limits of Philosophy*, edited by Richard Shusterman, 197–221. Oxford: Blackwell, 2004.

———. "Pragmatism: An Old Name for Some New Ways of Thinking?" *Journal of American History* 83, no. 1 (June 1996): 100–138.

Knapp, Kathy. "Richard Ford's Frank Bascombe Trilogy and the Post-9/11 Suburban Novel." *American Literary History* 23, no. 3 (Fall 2011): 500–528.

Kristeva, Julia. *Powers of Horror: An Essay on Abjection*. New York: Columbia University Press, 1982.

LaCapra, Dominick. *Representing the Holocaust: History, Theory, Trauma*. Ithaca, NY: Cornell University Press, 1994.

Lasch, Christopher. *The Culture of Narcissism: American Life in an Age of Diminishing Expectations*. New York: Norton, 1991.

Lefebvre, Henri. *The Production of Space*. Oxford: Blackwell, 1991.

Levin, Jonathan. *The Poetics of Transition: Emerson, Pragmatism and American Literary Modernism*. Durham, NC: Duke University Press, 1999.

Leys, Ruth. "The Affective Turn: A Critique." *Critical Inquiry* 37, no. 3 (Spring 2011): 434–72.

———. *Trauma: A Genealogy*. Chicago: University of Chicago Press, 2000.

Lyons, Bonnie. "Richard Ford: The Art of Fiction 147." *Paris Review* 140 (Fall 1996): 43–77.

Majeski, Sophie. "Richard Ford: The *Salon* Interview." July 7, 1996. http://www.salon.com/1996/07/07/interview_18/.

Marx, Leo. *The Machine in the Garden: Technology and the Pastoral Ideal in America*. Oxford: Oxford University Press, 1964.

Matthiessen, F. O. *American Renaissance: Art and Expression in the Age of Emerson and Whitman*. Oxford: Oxford University Press, 1941.

McCabe, Colin. "Realism and the Cinema: Notes on Some Brechtian Theses." *Screen* 15, no. 2 (Summer 1974): 7–27.

McCarthy, Thomas. *Ideals and Illusions: On Reconstruction and Deconstruction in Contemporary Critical Theory*. Cambridge, MA: MIT Press, 1991.

———. "Ironist Theory as a Vocation: A Response to Rorty's Reply." *Critical Inquiry* 16, no. 3 (Spring 1990): 644–55.

———. "Private Irony and Public Decency: Rorty's New Pragmatism." *Critical Inquiry* 16, no. 2 (Winter 1990): 355–70.

McGurl, Mark. *The Program Era: Postwar Fiction and the Rise of Creative Writing*. Cambridge, MA: Harvard University Press, 2009.

Mead, George Herbert. *Mind, Self, and Society*. Chicago: University of Chicago Press, 1967.

Miller, J. Hillis "Narrative and History." *ELH* 41, no. 3 (Autumn 1974): 455–73.

Mitchell, Juliet, ed. *The Selected Melanie Klein*. London: Penguin, 1986.

Mitchell, W. J. T. "Intellectual Politics and the Malaise of the Seventies." *Salmagundi* 47/48 (Winter/Spring 1980): 67–77.

Monda, Antonio. *Do You Believe? Conversations on God and Religion*. New York: Vintage, 2007.

Mouffe, Chantal, ed. *Deconstruction and Pragmatism*. London: Routledge, 1996.

Nadel, Alan. "The Integrated Literary Tradition." In *A Historical Guide to Ralph Ellison*, edited by Steven C. Tracy, 143–70. Oxford: Oxford University Press, 2004.

Nochlin, Linda. *The Body in Pieces*. London: Thames and Hudson, 1994.

Nussbaum, Martha. "Sophistry about Conventions." *New Literary History* 17 (1985): 129–39.

O'Connor, Brian, ed. *The Adorno Reader*. Oxford: Blackwell, 2000.

Phillips, Adam. *Winnicott*. London: Penguin, 2007.

Poirier, Richard. *Poetry and Pragmatism*. Cambridge, MA: Harvard University Press, 1992.

———. *The Renewal of Literature: Emersonian Reflections*. New York: Random House, 1987.

Posnock, Ross. *Color and Culture: Black Writers and the Making of the Modern Intellectual*. Cambridge, MA: Harvard University Press, 1998.

———. *Philip Roth's Rude Truth: The Art of Immaturity*. Princeton, NJ: Princeton University Press, 2008.

———. "The Politics of Pragmatism and the Fortunes of the Public Intellectual." *American Literary History* 3, no. 3 (Autumn 1991): 566–87.

Poster, Mark, ed. *Jean Baudrillard: Selected Writings*. Stanford, CA: Stanford University Press, 1988.

Putnam, Hilary. *Realism with a Human Face*. Cambridge, MA: Harvard University Press, 1990.

———. *Reason, Truth and History*. Cambridge: Cambridge University Press, 1981.

Putnam, Robert D. *Bowling Alone: The Collapse and Revival of American Community*. New York: Touchstone, 2001.

Ramazani, Jahan. *Poetry of Mourning: The Modern Elegy from Hardy to Heaney*. Chicago: University of Chicago Press, 1994.

Rebein, Robert. *Hicks, Tribes and Dirty Realists*. Lexington: University Press of Kentucky, 2001.

"Richard Ford on *Lay of the Land* Part 2." YouTube. March 2, 2011. http://www.youtube.com/watch?v=8xWgp9TjxDA.

Richardson, Joan. *A Natural History of Pragmatism: The Fact of Feeling from Jonathan Edwards to Gertrude Stein*. Cambridge: Cambridge University Press, 2007.

Rorty, Richard. *Consequences of Pragmatism*. Minneapolis: University of Minnesota Press, 1982.

———. *Contingency, Irony and Solidarity*. Cambridge: Cambridge University Press, 1989.

———. "Deconstruction and Circumvention." *Critical Inquiry* 11, no. 1 (September 1984): 1–23.

———. "Dewey between Hegel and Darwin." In *Modernist Impulses in the Human Sciences, 1870–1930*, edited by Dorothy Ross, 46–68. Baltimore, MD: Johns Hopkins University Press, 1994.

———. *Essays on Heidegger and Others*. Cambridge: Cambridge University Press, 1991.

———. *Philosophy and Social Hope*. London: Penguin, 1999.

Sacks, Peter M. *The English Elegy: Studies in the Genre from Spenser to Yeats*. Baltimore, MD: Johns Hopkins University Press, 1987.

Schoenbach, Lisi. *Pragmatic Modernism*. Oxford: Oxford University Press, 2011.

Seltzer, Mark. "Wound Culture: Trauma in the Pathological Public Sphere." *October* 80 (Spring 1997): 3–26.

Shoup, Barbara. "Interview with Richard Ford." *Other Voices* 31 (Fall/Winter 1999), http://webdelsol.com/Other_Voices/FordInt.htm.

Sprinker, Michael. "Criticism as Reaction." *Diacritics* 10, no. 3 (Autumn 1980): 2–14.

Strout, Cushing. *The Pragmatic Revolt in American History: Carl Becker and Charles Beard*. New Haven, CT: Yale University Press, 1958.

Taylor, Ronald, ed. *Aesthetics and Politics*. London: Verso, 1980.

Tompkins, Jane P. "Graff against Himself." *MLN* 96, no. 5 (December 1981): 1091–96.

Tracy, Steven C. *A Historical Guide to Ralph Ellison*. Oxford: Oxford University Press, 2004.

Trilling, Lionel. *The Liberal Imagination: Essays on Literature and Society*. Oxford: Oxford University Press, 1981.

West, Cornell. *The American Evasion of Philosophy*. Madison: University of Wisconsin Press, 1989.

Whicher, Stephen. *From Freedom to Fate: An Inner Life of Ralph Waldo Emerson*. Philadelphia: University of Pennsylvania Press, 1953.

White, Hayden. *Figural Realism*. Baltimore, MD: Johns Hopkins University Press, 1999.

Wideman, John Edgar. "Love and Truth: Use with Caution." *New York Times*, September 20, 1987.

Wilde, Alan. *Middle Grounds: Studies in Contemporary American Fiction*. Philadelphia: University of Pennsylvania Press, 1987.

———. "Strange Displacements of the Ordinary: Apple, Elkin, Barthelme and the Problem of the Excluded Middle." *Boundary 2* 10, no. 2 (Winter 1982): 177–99.

Wood, James. "Human, All Too Inhuman." *New Republic*, July 24, 2000, 41–45.

Wood, Michael. "Stories Full of Edges and Silences." *New York Times Book Review*, April 26, 1981.

Woolf, Virginia. *A Woman's Essays: Selected Essays*, vol. 1, edited by Rachel Bowlby. London: Penguin, 1992.

Ziff, Larzer. *Literary Democracy: The Declaration of Cultural Independence in America*. New York: Viking, 1981.

INDEX

THE NEW AMERICAN CANON

Violet America:
Regional Cosmopolitanism in U.S. Fiction
since the Great Depression
by Jason Arthur

The Legacy of David Foster Wallace
edited by Samuel Cohen and
Lee Konstantinou

American Unexceptionalism:
The Everyman and the Suburban Novel after 9/11
Kathy Knapp

Pynchon's California
edited by Scott McClintock and John Miller

Reading Capitalist Realism
edited by Alison Shonkwiler and
Leigh Claire La Berge